HAITHAM

Autobiography

NO ONE MAY REMAIN

AGATHA CHRISTIE, COME, I'LL TELL YOU HOW I LIVE

TRANSLATED BY NICOLE FARES

Haitham Hussein

No One May Remain (Autobiography)

The original project in Arabic was accomplished with the support of
Ettijahat-Independent Culture and the Goethe Institute
and was published by Mamdouh Adwan Publishing House

Translated by: Nicole Fares

United Kingdom
60 Blakes Quay
Gas Works Road
RG3 1EN
Reading
United Kingdom
info@dararab.co.uk
www.dararab.co.uk

First Edition 2021
ISBN 978-1-78871-081-7

Text Edited by: Marcia Lynx Qualey
Text Design by: Nasser Al Badri
Cover Design by: Hassan Almohtasib

To

My parents, who suffer the bitterness of asylum and alienation in their homeland.

Contents

Personal Note

I find myself connecting with the English novelist Agatha Christie (1890-1976), who I address in my soliloquies because of the warning she delivers to her readers in the introduction to her published journals, *Come, Tell Me How You Live.* The chapters that follow detail her life in the 1930s in the Syrian city of Amuda and in other neighboring cities, while traveling with her husband, the British archaeologist Max Mallowan (1904-1978).

In an effort to spare her readers disappointment, Christie forewarns that her book is not deep, nor does it elucidate the science of archaeology from any new or interesting perspective. It provides no beautiful descriptions of landscapes, nor does it remark on economic problems or ethnic matters. It discloses no historical details, either. Indeed, she describes the work as "a small beer—a very little book full of everyday doings and happenings."

And perhaps I should do the same.

I find myself agreeing with Amin Maalouf's introduction to his book *Disordered World,* in which he makes clear that he will not be addressing different disorders in separate chapters, neither independently of one another nor in any specific arrangement. He explains that his approach "will rather be that of a nightwatchman in a garden in the small hours after a storm when another more violent storm looms on the horizon. With his lantern, this man carefully picks his way, shining its beam first on one flower bed, then another, exploring one path, then retracing his steps and bending over to inspect an old uprooted tree. Then he makes for a promontory, puts out his light and tries to take in the whole scene."

I also find myself embodied in some form in Zygmunt Bauman's (1925-2017) description of the exiled in his book *Liquid Modernity*, as "one that is *in*, but not *of* the place," that they are suspended in a place where time has stopped, such that they are not fixed but not mobile, and not among the people of strength, nor among the people of travel.

I often feel the same. I find myself *of* the place but not *from* it, in it and not in it, as though I were hanging in a void, swinging as time slips and dissipates. I travel in my mind and memories, dive inwardly, hoping to reconcile myself and my surroundings. And as I intersect with the past and present, I ask myself a question that permits no evasion or overinterpretation: Have I found myself?

Will I find myself as I write this?

I am overwhelmed by questions that probe the relationship between the author, his self, and his writing, as well as with the characters he creates. To what extent can the author be free of himself before he withdraws into himself completely? And to what extent can he acknowledge reality and facts when he is used to bending them to suit his characters? What is reality vs. fiction in anything an author writes, aside from his autobiography?

And what is it, exactly, that we try to record? Is it ourselves or the lives of others, intertwined with our own? Why must we rush to document history? And why must we impose on the genre of biography the burden of documentation, to bind it with the chains of testimony, evidence, and truth? Where does documentation start and fabrication end in the world of the author-as-biographer? Why do we write at all? Is it to slip our ruses and truths under the cover of art? To flee? From whom and to whom? And why must we be entirely nude and demasked? Is there a stable place between pain and delusion? Is the novelist required to be cruel in describing facts and opening the reader's eyes? And why? Isn't such an attempt to illuminate pathetic, seeing as the writer himself is stumbling in the darkness, in search of light?

Some would prefer that literature were a method of restoration, a way of hiding flaws. They would prefer the author to pretend to live a perfect life, one of principles and ideals. They search out ways to lure people to their pages by guiding them, indirectly from afar, and by laying out tales of wisdom and parables, which in turn renders them uninfluential, unrealistic. But the principle of collision is a must.

The author needs to sprinkle salt over the wound in order to keep up a constant due diligence, so that his written word can be a meeting point, a path of reconciliation, a bridge of communication between oneself and the other.

What could a novelist write about while sitting in his shell, a martyr and a witness to the rampant ruins before him? He moves with the echo. The novel remains his trick, his game, and a sanctuary where he spends his day enthralling bored people who seek entertainment in horror stories. A novel is an internal revolution and an explosion in the darkness. It is a demonstration of suppressed intentions and desires, a weapon to challenge the devastation of souls. A liquidation of sorts: to progress to firing bullets of hatred and revolt onto the paper in an attempt to avoid collision and destruction in one's reality.

It is no secret that writing under immense pressure can spread confusion, because the angle of view is so narrow, and it's limited to certain distances and dimensions. Many dark aspects remain hidden from the writer, which keeps his work full of gaps, his book a castle long abandoned.

What could a writer do with such devastation?

Homeland has become a contemporary slave market. The revolution, a black market. The endeavor was to pollute those who had not yet been contaminated, so that their choice would fall between murderers and criminals—between the lesser of two evils. And each side presents itself as the savior. The rubble of tyranny must be discarded by shoveling its remains away from those chanting tired slogans.

Blood, souls, slogans, wagers, cities, and anything else one can remember are found in the world's markets, as tools for bargaining and as goods for trade. They are kept on the shelf for negotiation. They are only, it seems, considered a means of bringing players to the table to discuss prices.

The homeland is a battleground for killers. A country for rent. This is where we are headed. Countries are moving backwards, toward their pasts. How can we weather these rotten markets when we carry the heavy burdens of ignorance, delusions of grandeur, and exceptionalism?

Empty the cities of their people, redraw the maps and the boundaries between them. This is a new form of wicked engineering employed under the pretext of a plan to retrieve some lost paradise. This revolution is nothing but an Olympics of martyrdom, and everyone except martyrs must cross through the market swamps, guarding the gates of nothingness.

A refugee's life has become a Russian doll that restores its ordeal and mutilated copies, replicating the same successive tragedies, again and again. My family has become a global one, spread out over several continents and in many countries between East and West. I have a sister in Sweden, two in Turkey, one in Iraqi Kurdistan, and a fifth in Syria. I have a brother in Austria, another in the Emirates, and a third in Turkey. My mother and father have remained in Syria. And I am here, in Britain.

Each time I try to plan a family reunion, I quickly realize how impossible it is. I remember when we were young and would gather at the dinner table, quarreling and teasing each other. This is but a distant memory now—a dream. I tell myself that the mere thought of arranging a family reunion would be futile, a waste of time. But I comfort myself with the thought that we are one of the lucky among displaced Syrian families. Other families were decimated by the war. That is a great tragedy.

I search for positive ways to see this terrible displacement we Syrians have been subjected to, and I find myself happy. My happiness, however, is tainted with a bitter sorrow. I have known many unfortunates in Syria, victims of ignorance and poverty. They were victims, that is, until they left with their families for Europe, where they found refuge from the war, and also from ignorance and poverty. These people exchanged destitution for a comfortable future for their children. For them, the war was a blessing... in a way.

War has its blessings and fate has its mockery!

There were many experiences I wanted to write about and many stories I wanted to document, but I found myself taking other paths, picking up different stories and exploring what lay beneath them. One incident dug itself deeply into my life, my body, and my memory, and I remain unable to face it. More than seventeen years have passed since I had to endure the burn of my compulsory military service in Syria. I still can't put that experience into words. I relive the fiery pain whenever I try to document that bitter experience, and so I postpone writing about it, until maybe I can find a way to reconcile my memory and my pain. I also avoid incidents in which others bear some responsibility. I don't want to cause anyone any embarrassment, so I postpone writing about such things. Maybe I ought to flesh out the details in such stories? Perhaps, in doing so, I will be able to relieve myself of the burdens transferred onto my fictional characters.

Aren't we the inhabitants of our dark inner caves? Are we not trying to free the genie from its bottle? To allow it to express obsessions and desires, then stand before it and watch its revolution, its departure and liberation? What is this revolution we hope for? And what liberation do we imagine?

A motherland. What is a motherland? Is it possible to define what hardly ever requires a definition?

A pile of stones, streets, a handful of homes, poverty, hunger, homelessness, alienation, dispossession, misery, humiliation, imprisonment. A gambling table, a matchbox, a gunpowder warehouse...

In exile, one question persists on our minds—the question of the homeland. The sense of belonging we seek and the security we dream about.

In escaping our homeland, we may end up finding it. Exile introduces us to a belonging to the self and to others, to a distance that becomes a way to get closer to others, become more familiar.

Sometimes, the homeland becomes a veil, and exile becomes a mirror and a way home.

A real homeland is wherever one finds a moment of peace, a sincere smile, a deep sleep, a comfortable bed, a longing for tomorrow that replaces fear, the shiver of a lover, and an eagerness to see a loved one. Such simple details build a true homeland.

For us refugees, longing for home is key. The main subject of our analysis and research is still the missing spirit that was once inside us, back when we lived in our old homes. Each sentence ends with a groan and a sigh of sorrow. Our attempts to define anything are met with failure, since we lack self-consciousness. We used to miss belonging to a stolen homeland, but now we miss ourselves and draw strength from our opaque future.

Are You Happy To Be Here?

My dear Agatha, were you happy here? Were you happy there? Were you happy in your life?

You have written in your book about this part of the world: "For this is a simple, and, I think, consequently a happy part of the world. Food is the only consideration. If the harvest is good, you are rich. For the rest of the year there is leisure and plenty, until the time comes to plough and sow once more."

You affirm that it is difficult for people like you, who write Western thoughts about the importance of life, "to adjust one's thoughts to a different scale of values. And yet to the Oriental mind it is simple enough. Death is bound to come—it is inevitable as birth, whether it comes early or late is entirely at the will of Allah. And that belief, that acquiescence, does away with what has become the curse of our present-day world—anxiety. There may not be freedom from want, but there is certainly freedom from fear. And idleness is a blessed and natural state—work is the unnatural necessity."

You point out that you began writing your non-chronological diaries before the war, but that, four years after the war ended, your thoughts kept carrying you back to the days you spent in Syria, compelling you to extract your unfinished notes and journals and complete what you had started, then left unfinished. You say it is good to remember such days and places—and in that precise moment, the marigold hill bloomed, and old men with white beards walked behind their donkeys, perhaps entirely unaware that a war went on.

So I ask you these questions about happiness that I am sometimes asked as well:

Were you happy to be here? Were you happy in Edinburgh? Were you happy to have made it to Britain and saved yourself and your family from war? Were you happy in your life?

I am sometimes asked such questions by strangers I have only just met. They ask about my native country and its welfare, and the word "Syria" calls to their minds horrible images. They usually wonder at how happy I must feel to be away from such a country. They ask about my happiness as though I should feel blessed by my separation from my country.

And while I have no intention of depressing these strangers with my answers, I am unable to deceive myself. So I draw a smile on my face that I hope is hard to read, even if the sadness in the eyes of an immigrant cannot be masked.

Is it even possible to answer a question about happiness with a yes or no?

When pressed for an answer, I evade it. Instead, I debate the meaning of happiness. I tell them that happiness is man's impossible dream. That there are happy moments a man can steal from his reality, but that these moments can have no serious impact on one's life. These moments transform into yet another kind of happiness when they turn into happy memories that provide joy and hope through life and its surprises.

I tell them that happiness is relative. At times, I feel happy after hearing good news—a rare occurrence these past few years—or after certain situations end well. But this happiness is relative, in that it does not affect the trajectory of my life, nor does it shape or enhance the happiness one considers when discussing life. That happiness is an imagined romance.

I find myself ruining their discussion by turning it philosophical. I live my truth and refuse to falsify. I don't dilute or obscure language and ideas, and I ensure that my language is an arrow aimed straight at the heart of a truth I believe. Truth, in turn, is relative, changing from one person to another. The truth of happiness is something a person imagines, lives, and searches for.

When I turn the tables and ask the same question of my interlocutor, their discomfort, confusion, and embarrassment are palpable. I have returned their grenade of imagined happiness, now missing its safety pin.

"Are you happy?" The answers I receive are laced with sadness and confusion, given by people whose eyes avoid confrontation. They prefer to be the one doing the asking, their questions a burning coal that takes life for granted.

In schools here, students are often expected to express how happy they are. I sometimes take joy in annoying my daughter by asking her such questions as, Are you happy? She answers with a childish innocence I adore: Yes, I'm happy. And so I repeat the question and she answers, quickly growing bored: I'm happy... happy. And when I ask her: Are you sad? Angry? she answers me angrily: I'm happy, Daddy! So I ask her: Are you angry? And she screams at me: I'm happy—please leave me alone!

I have no doubt that education differs greatly between here and there. Growing up in an environment that discouraged me from expressing my feelings is probably why I have a habit of internalizing them. In my culture, if you're happy, you must not show it for fear of attracting the envy of others. Talking about your happiness could also cause bad luck, which could sour your happiness. And if you're sad, you must conceal your sadness, so as to not become a source of pity and weakness, and to avoid attracting criticism.

There is a saying here, that happiness is a habit. The more you repeat to yourself that you are happy, the more your negative emotions will decrease, and the more you will find yourself enrobed in positivity.

Some think I might encounter the Loch Ness monster in Edinburgh and document my sighting, then ask the creature to grant my wishes. Or that I might encounter William Wallace, who appealed and dazzled in *Braveheart*, as played by Mel Gibson. There is no limit to people's belief in superstition. And in this world, there is no one specific place for superstition. Myth passes through all histories, eras, and geographies.

I remember, Agatha, what you said in your journals about the concept of happiness in our regions at the time you were there: "For this is a simple, and, I think, consequently a happy part of the world. Food is the only consideration. If the harvest is good, you are rich. For the rest of the year there is leisure and plenty, until the time comes to plough and sow once more." I believe deeply that such times, with their ideas and beliefs, are gone forever. And that misleading happiness has been dissipated by virtue of many details, many developments, much violence and blood.

Is happiness a question or a dream? Isn't it the objective of everyone's dreams?

I must be happy, from the point of view of the one asking. And I'm aware of the reasons they give themselves for assuming my answer before it leaves my lips, presuming it must be so.

But in truth, I am not happy. And when I say I'm not happy, it doesn't mean that I'm sad or depressed. I am moving through the cycle of life and time. I experience fleeting moments of relative happiness and long dry spells of dullness amid life's routines and details that leave no room to contemplate either happiness or sadness. Emotions lose substance. Apathy almost always prevails, and I find myself avoiding deep excavations or questions about the truth of my feelings toward life, reality, and my past.

My happiness is in the small details. When I take my daughter to kindergarten and she sings along to the Fairouz songs I play in the car. When she leaps up and points out the different things we see along the way. When she looks for the moon, then finds it and tells me, happy to share her findings. When she runs in front of me and asks me to catch up. When she jumps on the lines drawn in the schoolyard and asks me to do the same. When she makes me promise to get her chocolate on our way home...

I am happy when I put my daughters, Heve and Roz, to sleep. They ask me to read them a story. Between passages, they tell me, "I love you, Baba."

The Curse of Alienation

You stutter. You hesitate before approaching the passport control counter, busying yourself with your bag, then taking refuge in the bathroom to ease some of the stress that shows on your face. You try to delay the inevitable. You're here to turn yourself in to the authorities and apply for asylum. You're aware that you've entered the country illegally and have broken the law, so you feel like a criminal. Now, how do you move past your nervousness and confusion to reach the other side? How do you embark on a new journey to a hopeful future?

Others entered from the sea, fortunate to narrowly escape the death that awaited them at its bottom. They slipped through the hands of slave traders and saw whales devouring their friends and companions.

Others entered over land, traversing several countries, taking risks and living horrors, fighting this journey of death to seek a free and dignified life in a world they assumed would welcome people from a world so different from their own. Theirs was a world left behind when it became too difficult to survive in. They were forced to leave, but continued to watch their country from afar, seeing a ball of flame that burned everything within it and everything that made it.

There are many ways of seeking asylum, but the goal remains the same: to reach safety after a long struggle and much suffering. To escape the inferno of death in its many forms.

What does a refugee call himself in the country of asylum? This is another dilemma that faces him. He had left a country that rejected him, that gave him no choice but to leave, and escaped to a country that welcomed and provided him with the means to live. A country that tried to prepare him for the future, so that he might benefit his new society and contribute, in turn, to its prosperity. In so doing, he would not become a burden on his society, avoiding his responsibilities or seeking ways to evade them.

What is a refugee? Is he an immigrant, an exile, an expatriate? Or is he living temporarily in another country, until the situation in his own is resolved? The refugee faces the dilemma of defining himself *to* himself, as well as to those around him. If he sees himself as an immigrant, his new country will never become a homeland, nor will it replace his previous country. And if he continues to see himself as an immigrant, he will soon erect borders to separate himself from his surroundings and his new world, and he will remain distanced, late to integrate or perhaps never desiring integration.

As for his feelings of exile, they play an unfortunate role in keeping his country attached to his soul, living in his conscience. The feeling of exile never leaves him, and he will forever look at the world through the eyes of a stranger who does not want to assimilate into that world and may even become hostile to it.

Definitions and descriptions of the state of a refugee are uncertain and controversial. The varying sentiments, goals, and visions give birth to more definitions, like branches of a tree. The country of asylum could remain a temporary station for the refugee. He could spend the rest of his life there as a visitor, never the settler-resident, and this will be reflected in his interactions with others.

The story of any refugee is not very different from the stories of other refugees. Dreams lead them on their way, even if the details vary. A fugitive from war is not like someone who escaped his country's deteriorating economic conditions, and not all refugees belong to the category of those seeking riches or the European paradise they've always imagined.

When a refugee enters a new country, they are both laden with preconceived judgements and driven by great illusions and dreams—that quickly shatter when met by reality. A refugee realizes he is not in the paradise he'd imagined, but rather in a country with divergent people and sentiments. The ways people view him differ, too. Some see him as a burden and a dependent, while others see a color or another diversity to add to their already colorful country.

A Series of Bitter Waits

She fell into the trap of bitter waiting, like a chain floating in a vortex, or a cursed maze.

I arrived at Heathrow airport and requested protection for myself and my family. They told me that they would consider providing protection for me, but not for my family, since I was physically present in their country, while the rest of my family was elsewhere.

Maybe I was lucky to have come by plane, landing directly at the airport without going through any of the many death stations and deadly sea trips. Perhaps, since I arrived in Britain shortly before asylum-seeking became more complicated, others now envy me.

All refugees are guided by shared dreams, uniting around the desire for a sanctuary that will enable them to live out the remainder of their lives away from the death in their country.

In the airport's temporary detention room, there was a small library that displayed children's books and scripture in multiple languages. Time felt heavy and stubborn. From that moment, I became a prisoner of endless waiting. Asylum can be described as a renewed series of long waits, followed by more waiting, and preceded by waiting, too.

I did not consider myself a refugee, an immigrant, an exile, or an expatriate in the countries I crossed and the cities I stayed in for different periods of time: from Dubai to Beirut to Cairo to Istanbul. There, I did not think of defining myself. But that changed when I arrived in Britain. Here... who am I? What am I?

Equipped with a modern cultural perspective and burdened with preconceived takes and perceptions, I claim to know this country partly through history, arts, and literature, and partly through the colonial legacy that remains present in my every thought and interaction. Where to start and where to go on my journey of discovery and expectation?

After being investigated at the airport, I was moved to a hotel near London. As it happened, it was the end of the week, so I remained there over the weekend, waiting for transportation to the temporary Wakefield camp in central Britain. The camp had a heterogeneous mix of refugees: from the East and West, Africans and Asians and others. Arabs made up the largest group of refugees. They came from many Arab countries, but mostly Sudan, Somalia, Eritrea, and Syria.

I met some people who introduced themselves as Syrians, but, after talking to them and asking about their homeland in attempt to get better acquainted, they looked unsure of their answers. When I told them that I could tell their accent wasn't Syrian, they claimed to have lived outside Syria for many years, then quickly relented and told me the truth: They were pretending to be Syrian to obtain residency, since the Syrian position was "better than theirs at the moment." In other words, the Syrian people's pressing concerns gave them a greater chance of obtaining residency.

There were also Arabs from other countries who had gotten residency by pretending to have Syrian roots. There were Kurds from Iraq and Turkey who presented themselves as Syrian Kurds and got residency as Syrian without any proof of their Syrian identities.

The apprehension among the refugees was palpable. They hid personal details from one another. Suspicion and paranoia made them distrustful, wary of everyone they met, wary of discussing their ordeals on the path to seeking safety. In their tales, smugglers became heroes. Although usually smugglers are cursed, in these stories, they were thanked.

The refugee camp was like a large prison. The veteran refugees tried to guide the newcomers, telling them what to do and how the procedures would go, as well as about the routines of the camp. They also told stories of those who had come before them, and of the places they were sorted and transferred. They spoke as experts on matters that involved the country and its refugees, when in reality they, like everyone else, were waiting at the same doorstep to take their first steps out of the camp and into their new lives.

I transitioned from waiting for my departure to Heathrow to waiting for my transfer to the camp, and from the camp to the shared residence, and from there to the city I would choose once I had my residency. I spent a long time waiting to travel, waiting to be moved from one location to another. As for the other things I spent a lot of time waiting for, well, they involve a labyrinth of papers and routines that every refugee must endure.

After the first interview, which is a detailed investigation, there is a waiting period before the second. This is the most important interview, because this is when the investigator and the Ministry of Internal Affairs decide whether to grant you asylum or reject your application. During that time, you remain suspended in the sea of waiting, living with different people from different cultures and languages.

Waiting can last weeks or months, even a few years without any convincing justification for the delay. Some have their application approved and asylum granted and are able to bring their families over within a few months, while others wait for two or three years before they finish the procedures for residency, asylum, and family reunification.

While I waited to finish my asylum application, another kind of waiting weighed on me. My family was in Istanbul. I had left my pregnant wife and my daughter behind, because I couldn't take them on my search for asylum and a decent life. We were waiting for our second child, Roz, who I had yet to meet, and who was now a year and a few months old.

Every day, I waited for the mail. In our country, the postman was a thing of the past, but here, he had become important, a person I always waited to see. Every day that passed without an interview, while waiting for an answer, increased the pressure of alienation and disrupted normal life. When a person is preoccupied, they can't focus on creating a social life, and they keep their distance, not integrating into their new society.

Waiting often results in disappointment, especially when the longing for what comes next is so great. This has been true for me more than once. I waited for months for my residency, and, once I received it, I waited on the procedures for family reunification. I was shocked when I got a rejection. The reason was that the authorities were unable to verify that my family was truly mine. I had to take a DNA test to prove it, and then submit a new request in the hopes that, this time, my waiting would not climax in disappointment. Then, I would have to resort to courts and judges, as here, in Britain, the judiciary system has the final say, unlike in the countries we came from, where courts and judges were mere tools in the hands of the authorities.

I had prepared myself to receive my family and hug my daughters, and I was shocked when their trip was postponed. I tried to understand my dilemma, to contain the crisis that I was continually facing. I filled my time with reading and writing, learning the language and discovering the city and its people, its markets and details, but my mind was haunted by my troubles and my waiting, my stress and my worry.

During these long waits, local officials tried to embrace refugees, preparing activities and festivals to dispel feelings of alienation and to push them to get to know their surroundings. The church cooperated with the city, staging different activities and trips for refugees, attempting to foster a family atmosphere to lessen the pressures of alienation and suffering.

I am still waiting, and I will wait for the remainder of the time in my new city, Edinburgh, where I moved and where I have yet to grow accustomed to the strange moods of the weather, carrying an umbrella in my sleeve as the locals do. I wait, hopeful for a return to my country after the war ends. But this is a hope that is slowly fading, because I know that, by the time the war ends, I will have become a stranger to my country, and it will also be stranger to me. I am reminded of the Russian, Ivan Bunin, who lived in France. When Soviet writer Konstantin Simonov suggested he go home, he said: "Please understand me: it is difficult for me to return to my country an old man, all my friends and family now lie in their graves and I will walk there as though through a graveyard."

Now I embody this feeling.

Tests and Practices

We are the ones who change the locals' perception of us, leading them to question us and everything we say. This is what refugees often admit to each other in frank moments. Here, you may encounter someone who tells the authorities that he is married with children, so the authorities initiate reunification procedures, when in truth he is single and in the business of human trafficking. You meet people who bring their children to the country, and then their nephews, relatives, and neighbors, all under the pretense that these are their children. Some receive payment in exchange for bringing children into the country as their own and then, upon landing, the children inform the authorities that their real parents are back in their native country. The authorities are then forced to bring them as well.

Many are the tricks employed by refugees in countries of asylum—by those who think themselves savvy and take pleasure in outsmarting the system, and by others who consider this a business. They cause the locals to go from sympathizing with refugees—from seeing them with compassion, acceptance and protection—to aversion and skepticism. This also reflects poorly on many aspects of a refugee's life, and on future refugees, who will be victims of the malice of those who came before them. They are the ones who pay the fine for the others' malpractice.

Among the sayings I always repeat is: "A refugee is bad until proven otherwise," and "a refugee is good until proven otherwise." For a time, refugees and locals sway back and forth together. The refugee is subject to testing and remains under some sort of observation until he proves his competence and ability to coexist and accept others, to look at the country as his own rather than as a waypoint that doesn't concern him.

There are refugees who live in narrow shells. They reside in the cracks of their new society, hostile to its decisions. They feel they have a right to intervene in many matters and affairs, and they place themselves in the trap of comparison, differentiation, and superiority in order to meet their psychological need to play a role, or to feel an artificial or inflated sense of importance. They hold on to more customs and traditions than they ever practiced or followed when they lived in their own countries. Their reactions grow counterproductive, and they feel their identity threatened, so they begin to emphasize it and cling to it, preferring it to the identity of their new society.

They would even say, at some point, that they were granted asylum because these countries needed them, needed their skills and energies, and they would ignore the fact that such countries can import people with whatever skills they need. This heightened sense of importance makes them feel entitled to many rights without having paid a thought to their duties and obligations.

Attempts to integrate aren't limited to the desire to learn a country's language, but also encompass the refugee's effort to convey an appropriate image of his culture and people, so that his new country sees him as an asset and not a burden.

If a refugee fails to consider his new country as his permanent home, and himself as a true ambassador of his country and culture of origin, then he will remain a stranger, separate from society and its people. He will be haunted by his many illusions and great ills, which keep him from seeing reality as it truly is, holding him captive to his own fabrications and misapprehensions. In a way, he will fit the great eleventh-century Syrian philosopher-poet al-Ma'arri's definition of true imprisonment, which is: to be both confined to a place and also confined by one's blindness to reality and its obligations. This blocks and blurs a person's future in all its details.

There are also refugees who think other new refugees are using up all the available opportunities and privileges in their new country, which leads them to resent each other. They look at one another with a superiority that leads, ultimately, to racism. This can only be overcome through awareness and responsibility, and through the belief that the diversity of life, the meeting of nations and races in diaspora, results in the birth of a new human identity both for immigrants and for locals, united by a hope of a better future for themselves and their children.

Once you leave your country, every other country is an exile. This is a nagging truth that every refugee feels, but the challenge remains: How do you turn exile into a home, when your old home has turned itself into an exile?

Shredding the Masks

As I studied refugees and listened to their stories, I noticed that many of them stressed to me, during the lulls in their stories, the importance of keeping their names confidential. I didn't understand why they were afraid of their names being known. Was it the eternal terror that occupied their spirits, keeping them afraid of their own shadows, as the saying goes?

Their stories have become their treasures, keeping them warm when they get cold, and from these stories, they draw a force that gives them patience, a fuel that drives their chatter during gatherings. Their tales have become the fire of ardent spirits, or coals that shelter them against the frost of alienation, dispelling their phobia of loneliness and alienation. So they preserve these stories, and they guard them as though they were treasures carried from their homelands, that must be kept close to their hearts.

Some are eager to tell their stories in dull, intricate detail, reciting them as though presenting their listeners with great secrets. Yet they are reluctant to let me write the stories down. There are those who allow me to record parts of their stories, as long as I leave out their names. And there are those who assume I am documenting their stories so they can be used as lessons to others, so they let me write them down, but still stress the importance of keeping their names a secret, to spare them the tangle of interrogations and scandal.

When I first asked Ali (a pseudonym) to relate the story of his journey to asylum in Britain, he refused, saying he was neither merchandise, nor material for entertainment, nor did he exist to generate sympathy and compassion. He would not let himself be a boon to those who trade in human life under the guise of charity or human rights.

Ali boasts that he made it from Beirut to Britain in only sixteen days, his historic triumph. He assures me that he survived murder, death, and drowning on more than one occasion, both on the Libyan coasts and at sea. He insists his story is unique, his journey special and extraordinary, and that he cannot gift it to anyone, for fear that they would steal it and reap the profits.

He is surprised when I tell him that his story has neither adventure nor heroism, that it is no different from tens of thousands of other journeys made by desperate people who were escaping a hell that had driven them to an unknown they hoped would be more merciful than their stolen homeland. He argues that he is unique, since he embarked on an adventure at sea, surfed and sought life, sacrificing his own for a more hopeful one.

Abdel Karim, a father of three, the eldest of which is nine, is lonely and depressed. His wife left him straight after they landed in Britain. He said he never failed her as a provider, and that he fulfilled all of her needs when he was in Damascus. Yet she betrayed the years they shared together, the good and the bad, and slapped him with a divorce. Now, she lives in a large house with their children while he lives alone in a small house, spending his time ruminating on his alienation, depression, frustration, and despair.

Abdel Karim told me, "When I think about it, I want to tear out my hair. I regret bringing her here. I should have applied to bring my children and left her, heartbroken, over there by herself. I should have deprived her of the children for the rest of her life. But because I'm a kindhearted idiot, I brought her here, and now she's taking revenge on me for the past. It's not my fault that she's my first cousin and I had first dibs on her. I heard she was in a relationship with someone, so I cut it off and forbade her to see him. As her first cousin, I had a right to marry her. Our society gave me that right, through traditions and customs that have been passed down through the years. I have the right to impose my will on her. But now she's using the law here to corner me."

He went on, "Imagine! She took off her hijab and challenged my authority! She told me that she hated me so much she could hardly stand to live in the same house with me, or even look at me. But she didn't keep me from seeing my children, so she does have a good heart. But I have no idea who turned her against me like this, who tarnished my image in her eyes!"

He chuckled as he told me how pleased he was that, despite the harm she'd caused by deserting and divorcing him, his children were his by blood. He told me the story of a man who got a DNA test—which you had to do to provide proof in your application, so they knew your children were really your own. His wife greatly resisted the DNA test, and it was later revealed that his children were not his by blood. What fatal news, my friend joked, to discover that your children, who you raised and gave everything, and who you'd fought for all your life, were actually someone else's. He laughed in sorrow, pain, and pity for this man who was afflicted with the truth after all those years of marriage, fatherhood (or so he thought), great responsibility, homelessness, asylum, and suffering. He praised his wife for at least not cheating on him, because what was most important was that his children were his and not another man's.

The divorce rate for Syrian women has skyrocketed after their arrival in Europe, so I went to some divorced Syrian women I knew in Britain, to ask their opinions, and to ask about what had motivated them to seek a divorce. There seemed to be elements of the past influencing the present, as many had gotten married as a result of need and pressure. Some women hadn't made the decision to marry their husbands; the decision had been made for them by their families and economic hardship. Essentially, they accepted the first proposal that came along.

But here, the economic need for marriage disappeared, the family pressures from fathers and brothers dissipated, and the authority of the community dissolved. They felt they could choose their lives and perhaps even reset the trajectory of their lives in these new circumstances, in this environment in which they'd found themselves. Here, they had freedom and a government that provided them with accommodations, as well as expenses and economic aid. Thus, a husband was no longer needed to protect and provide. The two parties had become equals in rights and duties, and this provided women with strength, giving them back their voices and true personalities, which had withered and weakened in their homeland.

There are those who describe this phenomenon as a feminist revolution, arguing that this war, and the great ordeal of asylum, in addition to horrific homelessness, presents a historic opportunity for women to gain their freedom and achieve their desires. The change didn't necessarily begin when they removed and shredded their hijabs—that was merely the first of many broken chains that had held them captive in the prisons of their families or husbands, or as maids and concubines.

There are also some who consider women's demand for freedom, and their removal of the hijab, as a rebellion against the laws of society and of Islam, linking the women's conduct to centralized religious and social authority. These people hide behind their laws and criminalize women who seek the freedom to live their lives, the freedom to choose lifestyles that suit them on their way to potential happiness. Those women had curled up deep within themselves during their strange previous lives, grown bitter and lost, and asylum has given them a shovel to unearth their true selves and reveal their true personalities, a conduit to a reconciliation with their desires, dreams, and lives.

Perhaps one paradox is that this asylum is a test of love and understanding within families and between husbands and wives. What was built on a mistake will inevitably collapse, and it will not withstand the cruelty of alienation. What was established on a strong and solid foundation will withstand the hurricane of asylum, which takes years to subside. A refugee can engineer his new life according to any conditions and rules, but if it comes without love and dedication, families will be lost in the storm, children dispersed between fathers seeking past glories and mothers seeking imaginary future ones.

It seems the country of asylum is a new battlefield for refugees, a cold war between them and themselves. And like all ongoing and former wars, there will be no victor, but destruction on all levels. And so asylum unveils the facts of people's personalities, the real and new faces of people and their souls, the true essence of these men and women. This new life will force people to rip off the masks they have grown so used to wearing.

Her Majesty's Prison Wakefield

I stayed in a makeshift camp in the town of Wakefield for about two weeks, and I was shocked by the terrible building that faced our camp: the Wakefield prison.

I could hardly sleep at night when I learned that the prison was mere meters away from my room. I startled awake every other hour, wondering whether having this large prison opposite a camp that served as a waystation for refugees on their asylum journey in Britain was a coincidence, or whether it was meant as a warning to refugees at the beginning of their new lives, a way to show them how much better life in the camp was compared to life in prison.

The area around the prison and the camp seemed perfectly calm. I couldn't stop myself from thinking about the stories of the prisoners and their misfortunes. I came from a country where prisons were doors to nothing. Prisons were surrounded by walls of fear, terror, intimidation, and madness, meant to defeat a person and destroy his soul.

I remembered my nights in the military parole prison during my compulsory service. My battalion commander had ordered my imprisonment, and I felt an intense, oppressive humiliation. They wanted to make it clear that a prisoner was nothing but an object for their amusement and torture, and that a prisoner would spend his whole life in that swamp of humiliation. Even though those two guards had been fellow conscripted soldiers, they transformed into monsters as soon as the doors were closed on us in prison.

Although it lasted only a few nights, it was a terrible experience. I still feel shame whenever I remember it. I feel shame for belonging in some way to those executioners, stripped of their humanity, who became tools of oppression and abuse.

I remembered many prison testimonials from writers who were exposed to such cruel and brutal experiences. As I contemplated the towering wall, which was dotted with surveillance cameras, I tried to imagine what was behind it, and I shivered at the thoughts that blended reality with my memories of prison in a country famous for cruelty, immorality, and murder.

I tried to soothe my anger and indignation. I hurried to the library, where I found comfort and refuge, calming myself as I sat between the shelves, contemplating my present and my past, and also imagining contradictory futures. Was that the moment my disenchantment began? Was the camp a threshold for disenchantment, a gateway to the prison of asylum and the cell of alienation?

I didn't want to be a prisoner of any nightmare, horror, or reality. I tried to overcome the suspicions that the prison wall left in my soul. It confused me and rattled my aspirations, grounding my dream of relocating to an imagined paradise.

Prison puts an end to illusions. It makes a nest inside the mind, a constant presence. Memories of those first days are not forgotten. They are immortalized, much like my memories of the first days of compulsory military service. These stories will be told and repeated with passion until I age and my memory spreads thin, yet it will leave no room for forgetting, ignoring, or erasing them. Such are the early days of asylum, a lingering tattoo on the spirit and memory.

I try to reconcile the contradictions of life and assure myself that prisons are necessary institutions so that countries can maintain a balance. I imagine countries without prisons—places where a person might be cleansed of his brutality, where he could transcend the criminal spirit that beset him—but quickly realize that my visions are mere delusions, and these ideals might be described as madness. Yet madness is sometimes necessary to preserve something of prudence, and there is nothing wrong with perfect madness—as opposed to a destructive and criminal madness.

For some time now, I have been training myself to give up the evil spirit that inhabits man. I suppress the anger that sweeps through me, telling myself that I must show tolerance and forgiveness, not out of strength or weakness but out of necessity. When I feel anger or hatred, these feelings affect me greatly. They shake my soul, cause me to lose my balance, and send me off the road to security, into a trajectory of catastrophic loss.

I convince myself to turn away from those who offend me, as time will punish them in its own way. I believe in the lessons of time and its principles—that it is impossible for a person to escape punishment for a wrong they committed against another. I try to forget and deprive that flame of hatred and bitterness, in order to keep it from burning up my heart and soul and disturbing my days.

The new places in which I've found myself have led me to dig deep into my past, into the memories of sorrow, oppression, and waste that I carry, that weigh me down. I convince myself that my future needs me to relieve it of the burden of those grudges, sorrows, and tragedies, so I can cross into tomorrow with the fewest possible losses.

When one person hates another, or when hatred occupies his soul, he will be prey to anxiety. He will think of ways to inflict misfortune on those he views as enemies, and he'll even put his own plans on hold in order to devise ways of interrupting the plans of his enemies and taking revenge. Preoccupied with methods of evil, he'll fall into a trap set by malignant people who want to derail his life and keep him from advancing. They will want him to reflect their distortions. He can free himself from hatred only by ignoring his pain and letting time heal his wounds. It is true that time is the best medicine and treatment, the best physician.

I still remember a powerful verse by Gibran Khalil Gibran, from his incomparable poem "The Storms": "And the murderer of the body dies for his actions, but the murderer of the soul remains unaccountable." The wisdom of this poet shows that punishment is the crime, and that the murderer's crime ought to be his own punishment, gnawing bit by bit on his soul, until he is crushed and smothered under its weight.

The daily routine in the camp resembled a life in prison. Mealtimes were precisely scheduled, and allocations were distributed to the refugees. Courtesy and formality were as common as arrogance and rudeness. Some rushed for food in a disgusting manner, thinking themselves clever. These people were always hungry, never full.

I would hold my meal card and stand in line, waiting, practicing my hobby of studying people and their behaviors, how they entered the endless contests that constitute the Olympics of Life. I thought of the prisoners on the other side of the street, behind those high walls, and how they, too, would be waiting their turn to take their meals with discipline and restraint. Then I came back to the scene in the large dining hall and watched the refugees of different nationalities, the different ways they ate the food. I thought about how eating involves cultural habits that reflect an entire history, a life and its social and civilizational norms.

These refugees represented a mix of languages and peoples. Africans from different African countries kept to themselves. Iranians attached large crosses to their walls and looked down on others, feeling superior. They considered the other refugees in the camp part of a past they preferred to forget, now that they had converted to Christianity. Many insisted that these refugees changed their religion in order to obtain residency. The response to this rumor was usually that the church wouldn't benefit from opportunistic people who employed religion as a selfish tool, but it would benefit from the generations that followed, who would be raised as true Christians. Then there were the Arabs and Kurds who waged their unending political debates, and who looked at the opportunistic Iranians with disapproval, accusing them of switching religions as quickly as they changed their identities. Others would cling to their faith and flaunt it as a clear sign of their superiority to those who would convert to Christianity.

Some nights, I woke up terrified, remembering the shadows of the high walls around Wakefield prison and imagining ghosts pouncing on me in my room, which faced the prison. I tried to transform my panic into a joke. I told myself that the memories of my time in prison, and the disastrous, ghostly stories I had preserved, weren't enough to turn me into an anxious creature, haunted by fear. But then my first days of asylum came, and they added to my store of sorrow and fear, deepening my nightmares and paranoia.

This is how I dispel the fear that seizes me: I turn it into sarcasm, so that it loses its edge and meaning. I dismantle and strip it, so that I can see it as a mess, which I won't allow to unsettle my future.

The HM Prison Wakefield was one of the highlights in my journey to my new world. Its walls are stamped in my memory, and sometimes it morphs into a nightmare that recurs from time to time.

I welcome these new nightmares, which can't compete with the nightmares that occupy my mind and spirit.

Yorkshire Meadows

Perhaps it was Emily Brontë's *Wuthering Heights* that first inspired me to venture near the heights of Yorkshire's lawns in central Britain, between its forests and cliffs, where the awe of nature overshadows and glorifies everything.

I remember novels that immortalize their chosen settings. They highlight these places, and their impact on the characters creates a kind of identification between nature and humans. I wonder about the possibility of retracing the steps of fictional characters in real life, either for the sake of finding the imagined in reality or to find realism in the imaginary.

First published in 1847, *Wuthering Heights* remains a milestone in the history of English literature. It is the only novel written by Emily Brontë, one of the three Brontë sisters—Charlotte, Emily, and Anne—who wrote influential works while living in strange isolation. Charlotte Brontë wrote *Jane Eyre* and Anne Brontë wrote *Agnes Grey* and *The Tenant of Wildfell Hall.*

Wuthering Heights is set in the mid-nineteenth century, in a region where dispute and conflict prevailed. Emily Brontë's novel remains a source of inspiration and quotation for many works of art and drama. Brontë has inspired numerous works, including an award-winning 1939 film directed by William A. Wheeler.

Brontë depicts the kind of brutal and devastating love that shatters a man and drives him to take revenge on everyone around him. He eliminates everything that prevents him from communicating with his beloved, in a beautiful illustration of the brutal manifestations of human weakness. That weakness overflows with madness and destruction, leaving its owner a wreck, a shadow of a man who haunts the ruins of his soul, only to return once more to the place of his love and passion.

Brontë shows us the struggle between reconciling the past with its details and reliving it. In the case of her protagonist, Heathcliff, it's apparent that he has been living in the past since his sudden departure, which was no less surprising and strange than his return. She illuminates how some forms of love can kill, while others can destroy. She writes of various cases of murder and destruction that were motivated by love and a defense of love.

The end is an introduction to possible beginnings among the Heights. Heathcliff is hostage to Cathy's dead visage, which lives on inside him, and her melodious voice, which never leaves his hearing and imagination. His future stretches out, lonely and hollow without her.

I stand listening to the sound of the springs and to the silence around me in a place where huts scatter, where there are caves and trenches, and where wild animals seek refuge in their homes when threatened. I redraw the image of Heathcliff in my mind, a protagonist who on the one hand inspires sympathy and compassion, and on the other condemnation and accusation.

We were anxious from the start of our trip, which began on a cloudy morning. But after arriving at the Heights, the sun shone on us from between the passing clouds. And with the brightness of the sun, warmth seeped into our bodies. We sought shelter in the shade of the trees, but as soon as the sun hid again, we came out of the shade, seeking it. We continued to enjoy the moodiness of nature and its humor. With every change, God painted a new scene.

The volatile, stormy atmosphere is a feature of those highlands and meadows. We climbed a hill, crossed a river, enjoyed a waterfall and the dancing of the twigs and leaves that seemed to mimic the rapid movements of the springs around us. Blossoming buds announced the coming of an enchanting spring, a symphony of nature to set the soul and body at ease.

We passed lovers camping alongside the river. They were getting to know nature and adapting to it for days and nights. They fell into the footsteps of the novel's protagonists and lived alongside their unique stories and delightful adventures.

The path into the world of the novel is paved with tales and wonders. And the path into the novel's setting is no less enjoyable than the act of reading the novel. Here, real life and fiction meet, history and adventure overlap, and myths and epics are of equal importance, as they are often the highlight of our journey toward and among beauties.

Brontë has granted the ultimate heroism to nature, which polishes humans and shapes them in a way that suits the conditions in which they find themselves. Nature appears to be a partner in decision-making, or in sharing destinies and endings. And the Heights are not confined by geographical dimensions and natural topography. Their implications affect lives and express their sunken peaks and heights within hearts and souls. They are the partiality of mountains, the storm of imagination.

In Brontë's novel, every character reaches a new height, a new compelling climax, and a link in an endless series of towering high-rises of extreme impact and pain. Everyone is both a hangman and a victim. A monster and an angel. Love is the cause of utter devastation. Imagine an insane sort of love where someone kills their beloved in the name of love, while believing themselves to be the defender of that love.

Our short trip, which lasted a few hours, was a walk in nature and the contemplation of literature. During it, I was reminded of the questions that preoccupied me after I read the novel and watched more than one of the films it inspired. Could Heathcliff be classified as a murderous lunatic? Or could his crimes be justified as unavoidable reactions? Was Heathcliff lost before he met Cathy, or was he lost in that maze after meeting and loving her? Which of the two mazes was the fiercest and deepest? Did Heathcliff live in the Highlands, or did he become a prisoner of his own mind, only able to end his loneliness through death?

And perhaps the most persistent of my questions: How much injustice exists in nature, and how many anonymous, wronged lovers exist, like Heathcliff, their stories unknown?

Edinburgh Cannon

BOOM.

It is one in the afternoon, Edinburgh time. I have yet to get used to the ritual *bang* in this city. The cannon's sound and echo bring this place joy and transmit a sense of reassuring comfort to passersby. The listener doesn't need to look at his watch, because the timing is signaled to him by the cannon's firing. Yet you see, nonetheless, many automatically glance at their watches.

The sound of the cannon shook my being. For a moment, I thought I was back in Syria. I saw people around me enjoying the sun, relaxing on Princess Street as though they were at a beach on the Mediterranean. Here, a semi-naked beautiful woman lay on her stomach, reading a book as though she were alone in her bedroom. Her legs moved restlessly, and she seemed deeply absorbed in what she was reading, her enjoyment intense as she absorbed the book and the sun's rays.

Whenever I see a scene like this, I wonder what would happen if this scene were to take place in Syria? The woman would certainly be called a whore. Differing cultures overshadow all behavior and etiquette. Here, you choose to behave the way you think suits you, but there, you have to behave according to what is chosen for you, what is dictated for you, whether it suits you or not.

I haven't grown used to the sound of the daily cannon at the center of Edinburgh. Whenever I happen to be near the famous castle, I am startled by the cannon's thunder, which has been this city's daily ritual for many years. I cannot get used to what leaves a tingling in my soul, because my mind is filled with painful memories, and the sound of the cannon exhumes that rubble and fans its embers. It resurrects it and keeps it raging.

I remember when I was in Sharjah in October 2012. While in a café on the corniche by the lake, we heard the cheerful sounds of colorful fireworks, celebrating a holiday. For a second, I thought I was at home in Damascus, telling my family to stay safe and take shelter. We lived under the threat of bombs and the horror of skirmishes for months at a time. But here, people were happy to hear the fireworks, and they wore large smiles as they watched the extravagantly colored paintings in the sky. I pitied myself and wondered whether I would always be held captive by the fear of explosions. Would I ever overcome my current state?

Am I a creature of war who will never recover from his ills and wounds? Are my noisy memories bound by obsessions with war and the sound of gunfire?

It's been years since I ran from the war in Syria, but not a day passes when I don't recall it in one way or another. Before I was forced from my home, I finished writing *The Novelist Who Beats the Drums of War*. I wanted to put on paper some of the events that I had survived and witnessed, but I wanted to study the literature of war first. I wanted to see how other novelists dealt with war in their works, how they fought it with their literature, and how they warned of its madness.

Back then, when we saw dead bodies in the streets, which nobody dared remove or bury, we told ourselves that these were dark days that would pass and never return. And when events escalated into continuous nighttime clashes, we deceived ourselves, saying the morning would certainly bring good news, especially since international figures—presidents and kings—urgently demanded the removal of our criminal and his prisons. But when the bombing began, I knew I had to leave, and I realized that I would not return any time soon. Before that, I had convinced myself that the war would not last, that the modern world had moved past eras of total annihilation and grown inclined to peace. I had convinced myself that it was impossible for people to stay silent and ignore massacres for long.

I know now that I was a dreamer, romantic and naïve. Blood draws more blood, and entire cities can be obliterated. Millions of Syrians around the world are witness to the lies of their leaders, and they have painted their shames and horrors for the world to see. Promises of revenge doom the future.

I am haunted by the incessant pain and sounds of war inside me. After the weeks I spent in London—moving from home to home, staying with friends—I needed to be by myself and be one with myself. I had missed the intimacy of a room of my own and a bed, the warmth of which I could enjoy, and messy sheets I could leave behind when I got up.

They placed me in Edinburgh, in a palace overlooking the sea that dated back to the early nineteenth century. When I closed the door to my room, I threw myself on the bed and remained there for a few minutes, trying to draw in more air, trying to breathe normally. Perhaps when a person loses his place in the world, or becomes a nomad, he loses something of his psychological balance. I kept looking at the beach while I lay in my bed. The sounds that came from outside were a blend of birds chirping and seagulls squawking and the noise of squirrels moving lightly and quickly through the trees.

I was surprised by the open space on the city's main street. The Waverly train station stands between the two parts of Edinburgh. On one end is the ancient city, with its ancient ruins, the most famous of which are the historical castle and Royal Mile Street. These stand among many other ancient monuments in a city built in layers. And on the other end, there rises the new city, with its distinct characteristics.

I liked the broad warmth and beauty of the city center. I reminded myself that, if this city were in Syria, people would have long since defaced and distorted it with miserable commercial towers, or rented it to companies to bleed the city and its people dry.

I have a hard time trying to explain the relationship that grows up between a person and a city they love. Edinburgh is one of those cities that sneaks into your heart, until you find yourself suddenly attached to it, inhabited by its calmness, beauty, and familiarity, and the kindness and grace of its people. There, a new waiting period commenced. I entered the morass of routines, but with a new spirit, because I had gone from the asylum-seeking stage to the first steps of the refugee stage. That is, I took a step up the asylum ladder and rose in the ranks of refugees. My residency card was in my pocket, and I was proud of it. I applied for a passport, and when I received it three months later, I promptly applied for a tourist visa to Turkey, but was rejected.

By then, I should have grown used to disappointments. Everything seemed to come late to me. I got my residence papers after more than a year and a month of waiting, and my request to bring my family here was rejected the first time. It was another six months before I could bring them. Meanwhile, I waited a year and nine months to see my wife and my daughters, Roz and Heve.

Modern means of communication were not enough. There is no compensation for missing the embrace of a daughter who a father has yet to meet. There is no compensation for never playing with or spoiling that daughter. I saw Roz, who was born in the Turkish city of Batman, grow up in pictures and on video.

It had taken us more than four years to conceive our daughter, Heve. My wife had suffered several miscarriages, so the anticipation of our daughter's birth kept us excited and happy.

We had left our home in Damascus when my wife was in her first months of pregnancy, moving from house to house, from my family's home to hers, where she settled for the remainder of our displacement. My family housed more than twenty-five people—my sisters and their husbands and children—so the house was overcrowded. My wife needed a more comfortable space for the rest of her pregnancy.

At the same time, I was working to secure the papers I needed to travel from the Ministry of Education in al-Hasakah, Syria. Bribes opened doors that were shut, and I was able to travel to the Emirates, knowing that I wouldn't be able to come back to my country in the near future.

My friend Hassan Draei was the last person I said goodbye to in my city of Amuda. His son was the first person I met in Edinburgh. I owe Hassan a lot. He helped liberate me from my fear of breaking into the world of writing. He assured me that writing was our only way to live. My experience assisting him with his book, *The Burning Pillar*, strengthened my psychological defenses and eased my fear.

Memories sweep over me. I grab onto them, collect them, and scatter them here and there. I remember decisions I made and mantras I repeated to safeguard me against despair and weakness.

I have no doubt that those who are right don't wait for the recognition of others. Instead, they take their rightness into tomorrow, without fear of the accusations and suspicions they might face. Likewise, a talented person does not wait for acknowledgement of his talent. He must be confident enough to move into his tomorrow and create his fate. Only miserable people with no confidence and faith in themselves seek recognition and acknowledgment from others, who in turn keep them as dependent followers that they will, ultimately, betray.

Global Identity

Sometimes I joke to the people around me that, whatever country we end up in, it will be struck by a violent earthquake. I point out that, when we moved from our hometowns to Damascus, war followed us; so we left and headed to Cairo, where soon after the power struggle peaked. We made it out just before the June 30 coup. After that, our stay in Istanbul was temporary, pending our departure to Europe. Yet for my family, that temporary stay lasted three years.

I felt the years of my life seeping through my fingers as I waited. This is a temporary life. Here, the temporary refers to the chronic, to a constant state concealed as a temporary one.

I have met, and continue to meet, many people from both the East and the West who moved from their homelands to other countries and are obsessed with a hope of return. They believe that their stays in these new cities, which for some have stretched to years, are only temporary, and that it won't be much longer before they will, surely, go back to their homelands.

This presumed inevitability reflects an unintended fallacy, a deceit of the self, because time does not wait for one to complete his projects or meet his goals, nor for him to fulfill his dreams and accomplishments before returning him to his permanent life back home, where he imagines he will once again establish a new life, shaking off the dust of temporary residence, building a permanent life: one stable brick at a time. By then, time will have exhausted the man and kept him on the edge of life until he realizes that he has been the permanent resident of the place he saw as temporary. He has become a prisoner of his habits, a prisoner of a novel kind of alienation that he created to fool himself into believing he would move back, away from this diaspora that clings to him like seawater, in which he will forever swim.

When I asked my grandmother why my grandfather had bought a house on the northwestern edge of the city, she told me that he chose the place because it was close to his village, north of the border. From there, he could see the Mardin city lights as before. My grandfather used to say that their house made for a pretty good arrangement, because their stay was temporary and would not last long. His future plans—his permanent plans—were all imagined in that happy place: his village. Even on the cusp of his seventieth year, he still thought of his residence as temporary, that he would build a new beginning and seek permanence in Mardin someday soon.

Of course, my grandfather never did return to his village to be a hero and take back his land. His sons did not return to the village, either, and his grandchildren were displaced to many countries, where many of them carry similar feelings, that surely they will return to their lands and their dreams, that their stays are merely temporary. They see the lights of cities that were once shelters, that exiled their ancestors and made refugees of them, and these now call them to return, mirroring the delusions of the past.

There is both misfortune and consolation in the saying, "Work for your world as though you had never lived, and work for your hereafter as though you will die tomorrow." With such a focus on work, this saying injects a sort of imperative to work toward one's return to their permanent residence, to the place they desire. But this residence will be lost in the crowd of temporary residences. The dreaming generation will no longer be able to impose its visions and dreams on the generations that follow, who will find themselves the sons and daughters of a new place that their parents considered temporary. They will belong to it, and they will feel a sense of settled-ness in the place where their memories were made, where the fable-like stories in their memory take place. There, they build their permanent dreams, in the places their predecessors looked on as temporary waystations. And here, the struggle of place and time—of generations, dreams, and memories—goes on.

There are those who waste their lives in this trap of all that is temporary. They force themselves to play the role of guest, neglecting the duties they have toward their place and time. They stay ready to depart and, as a result, lose the connections that would have made this temporary location a permanent home and an alternative homeland. A return to that place where they believe their roots are would, in truth, be a kind of alien exile in itself, because by that time too much will have changed. Change affects everything.

Many refugees feel a sense of the temporary. This feeling dwells in them, occupies their dreams and, at times, causes them to lose their balance. They believe they will return to their homelands soon, always soon. But, in the meantime, they get used to their shelters and enter a cycle of daily routines, turning their deviation from assimilation into normalcy, so as to remain on the road to their imaginary life.

Some resent their refugee status and hold that feeling close to their hearts at all times. Alienation dominates their minds and souls, and they exclude themselves from reality under the pretext of not belonging. They fear losing their identities, personalities, and everything about themselves they consider unique and distinct. This feeling makes its way into their homes and every social circle, deepening and strengthening their loyalty to an anticipated return, which will never materialize because of the rift they have created between themselves and their present.

The present is sacrificed for a future that ultimately repeats the past. The one squandering his present doesn't feel that he is fighting the windmills of his delusions. He, who was once drowning in misery, stubbornly squanders his present and future in search of a promised glory.

I have met some Middle Easterners here in Britain who want the privileges of freedom, the support and protection of the government of their temporary residence, who don't hide their dissatisfaction with many things, behaviors and ideas. They criticize these things and try to change them. They fall into a trap of superiority reinforced by isolation and alienation, and they claim that they're protecting their identity, personality, and families from being erased. In truth, this attitude stems from fear of the self, fear of the other, and a lack of self-confidence. Thus, the refugee becomes lost in the idea of regaining permanent residence in a place that never satisfied him in the past, nor could it satisfy him now. He believes his country of asylum could change to match his dream and desires, which might content him in time.

Is engineering imagined refugee homelands around the world a new global trend? And is the participation of refugees a decisive factor in the development of a homeland in their minds? Was the participation of refugees from around the world in Brazil's 2016 Rio de Janeiro Olympics a step toward advocating for the refugee cause, or did it propose that asylum has become an alternative homeland for refugees, a transnational home that surpasses borders, time, and generations? Should this, then, not be considered an affirmation of the failure of international policies that claim to seek a solution to the crisis, to reduce refugeeism and address refugee issues?

There was a Syrian comedian in the seventies and eighties, Nihad Qali, who was famous for portraying a character called Hosni al-Bourdan. In one scene, al-Bourdan says that, if we want to know what's in Italy, then we must know what's in Brazil. That scene garnered superficial smiles and laughter.

By these lights, one can argue that nothing is outside the game of influence and self-interest played by those who buy the consciences of others and play God. A war that rolls across countries like a ball of fire always leaves behind people from different sides of the conflict, convinced that the reason they remain in foreign lands is to achieve an imagined victory for themselves, which will in turn cause a historic setback for the country and the people who took them in. And, if we really want to know what happens in the land of war and refugee outsourcing, then we must know what goes on with its allies, which manipulate peoples' fates, and what goes on in the slave markets—in other words, international politics—and with the great warlords who wear ties: weapons' manufacturers and international firms that trample everything in their path to make money regardless of the cost, be it more destruction, more wasted blood, more and more crime, which spawns yet more crime.

Today, the refugees scattered internationally have reached alarming numbers, triggering calls to protect countries from their influx. This has happened in some European countries, where there are proposals to erect walls that would limit the flow of refugees into those countries and protect people from the diseases these refugees carry. These calls cite the threat refugees pose to the characters of those countries, whether on national or religious grounds.

Must refugees bear the weight of such accusations? Why are refugees portrayed as assailants, threatening the safety of others? Were these refugees not themselves safe people once, in their own homelands, before dirty wars and masked conflicts toyed with their fates, stranding them and making them refugees? There is a spot-on Kurdish proverb that says, "Birds bond over the bread of the dervishes," meaning that people unite against a grave crisis afflicting their homeland and their dreams.

Why does the search for solutions to the refugee crisis continue, without any serious search for solutions to the wars and crimes that create refugees? It's as if the same doctor who pumps toxins into his patient's body also conducts experiments on how to cure him, and also regrets having to remove his organs to treat him. The doctor himself is the murderer. It is impossible for him to find a treatment or prescribe an effective medicine.

Could asylum be, in a sense, a global deal made and maintained in a black market, where money is hoarded and transferred on a global scale? On the other hand, is asylum a sort of alteration in the structure of some societies at the expense of others—the theft of human wealth under the guise of kindness? Has the modern world become a stage set for disappointment and defeat? Are companies and gangs controlling arms and seeking to hoard wealth, growing more criminal with the swift development of science and technology?

Do events that plague the modern world reflect directly in its culture, or do they need time to crystallize and mature before manifesting in artistic, cultural, and creative forms? Does this mean that culture is dependent on economies and politics, and that it traces their impact on all aspects of life? Might it then be said that culture has abandoned the role it was supposed to play as innovator, in favor of a dependency that does not suit its nature?

Is culture the last bastion of humanity, where silence is slowly seeping in? Or has it been, throughout history, a collage of diverse and contradictory perspectives on the issues it addresses? Where are the intellectuals situated in this global landscape, which appears at the height of its imbalance? Do intellectuals have any role in restoring equilibrium to a world steadily losing its balance, filled with statements of hatred and racism and the beating of war drums here and there?

Is there a way to mitigate the effects of intensifying wars, which create vast numbers of displaced people, both victims and refugees? How can intellectuals face this torrent of gunfire and buzzing of bullets with their pens, words, and peaceful behavior? How will intellectuals deal with the insanity of arrogance and the horror of aggression that threatens world peace? And can they defend against a superficial populism that exploits people's fears and terrors and weakens them, fostering an environment favorable to extremism—albeit with a slogan of democracy, human rights, and coexistence?

Will intellectuals become hostages to frustration and despair, or will they act against extremism and violence, raising their voices in support of just causes and in defense of human beings, regardless of their shape, color, language, or religion? Will culture regain its guiding role and spread enlightenment, curbing the wretched allegations that spread in the West about the backwardness of the East and its misery, and of the violent image it casts on religion, criminalizing millions of people with that image, thereby creating real violence to follow that which is imagined?

It is no secret that global polarization—in the realms of politics and economics—has direct and hidden impacts, with immediate or delayed effects on cultures around the world. One can see it manifest in many cases, showcased by global developments and changes that many large countries are undergoing, in addition to the developments taking place between East and West.

In Europe, which was once a center of illumination and enlightenment and a haven for civilization and progress, voices call for walls to be built on the borders of some countries. These loud voices come not from ordinary people but from leaders, under the pretext of addressing potential terrorism and preventing the arrival of terrorists, who might be in among the flowing waves of refugees. But reality suggests the opposite, especially when some leaders claim they fear for their countries' Christian identity, thus fueling religious conflict without contributing to dialogue. Statements, facts, and policies show a fondness for walls among right-wing politicians in both Eastern and Western nations.

Many new written works call for solidarity with refugees. The Western voice is more convincing to Europeans than the voices of Easterners, whose writings can be seen as biased toward their own people rather than presenting holistic visions of humanity.

Among the works that address the plight of Syrian refugees is *On the Run from Death* by Wolfgang Bauer, a German who attempted to document the stories of a group of Syrians and their attempts to cross into Europe. He writes of their exploits sailing from Egypt and Turkey and their encounters with blackmail and human trafficking, including falling prey to smugglers who lack consciences, who see only the potential money to be made.

Bauer's goal was to document the sensory experience and reconstruct the reality of what it means to flee and seek asylum. He noted the failure of the EU's policies to prevent undocumented immigration, and its inability to capture smugglers, despite strict measures on the Mediterranean borders, the recruitment of hundreds of thousands of soldiers, and their advanced military equipment. With bitterness and sorrow, he writes, "The Mediterranean that was the cradle of Europe and its birthplace has become a scene of failure."

At the end of his work, he calls for help: "How long must we wait while we watch these people drown on the high seas? How long must we force a young generation of Syrians to resort to illegal means and leave them to face human traffickers and gangs? How long will we keep betraying ourselves and laughing at them? Do not force women, children, and men to take refuge in boats of asylum and death. Open the borders now. Have mercy and show compassion."

No doubt such calls arise from a place of humanitarian feeling and a deep sense of responsibility and appreciation for people of different genders and colors. Yet it's striking how the call is to embrace refugees rather than to end what causes people to take to the seas, risking their lives in the hopes of salvation and the dream of a decent life.

Perhaps we must emphasize the importance of putting pressure on the source of the bleeding to stop the loss of so much history and so many people, rather than opening borders and enabling the causes of these refugees' displacement to remain unaddressed and therefore steadily worsen. Open borders will not stop ongoing crimes against millions of people, but instead will merely transfer the struggle from one location to another, redrawing the lines of fire and fanning the flames.

I believe there is an urgent need for the kind of books that Franz Kafka once spoke about: "What we need are books that hit us like a most painful misfortune, like the death of someone we loved more than we love ourselves, that make us feel as though we had been banished to the woods, far from any human presence, like suicide. A book must be the ax for the frozen sea within us."

I remember a passage I read in the novel *The Disappeared* by Kim Echlin, in which she writes, "The papers reported mass slaughter in your country. You traced your finger over the newsprint and said, 'Sometimes they write millions dead, and sometimes they write thousands. Don't they know? How can they sleep at night pretending to write facts when they don't know?'" Perhaps a large part of not knowing happens somewhere far away—the same place that lives inside me.

During my move from one country to another and between temporary residences, I came to realize that most people are led by a media that pollutes their minds and makes them submissive followers. The media conveys an image, news, and commentaries. The media imposes their own perceptions and pushes a strict way of thinking that builds a tunnel, after which they offer ways to help people escape the tunnel. The reporter chooses part of the image, creates a problem, and discusses it in relation to his proposals. He takes this partial image as a starting point without returning to the root of the problem, but rather seeking to discuss the problem's implications and supposed effects. Here, with a copy and in the absence of the original, he places importance on something one minute on something else the next to distract and delude. In practice, thinking is restricted. The path to a dead end has already been laid. The despair imposed is a game they play to manipulate peoples' minds.

Which Would You Choose?

Which method of murder would you choose? In that moment, all I could guess was that he meant to ask: Would you choose to die by ISIS machetes and knives, poisoned by hatred, sliced through the neck? Or a death by the bombs of Bashar al-Assad, which carry with them, in addition to explosives, a grudge against your country's history, geography, and people?

But because the British prefer to approach questions indirectly and evasively, the question lured me into a discussion of the situation in my country, Syria, the war there, and the British parliamentary vote, which had authorized their government to carry out specific strikes against ISIS following the seizure of Palmyra.

He asked me, If I had a choice between ISIS and the Assad regime, which would I choose? I looked deep into his eyes. He felt my accusatory stare at this hidden suggestion that I carry the seed of terrorism in my soul—a result of my upbringing under the oppressive Assad regime, or the product of a social system dominated by Islam. He asked without wondering whether I approved of the criminality and terror of one party or the other. He assumed that I'd pick a side, or perhaps he wanted to trap me in that choice.

When I lived there, in that country thousands of miles away, I had many stereotypes and prejudices about this place, the country where I now reside. This country, which has given me all the rights guaranteed by law to any British citizen. This country that has its rights and duties.

One stereotype entrenched in the circles in which I hung out was that sex was terrifyingly common. That people had sex in the streets, that one could join a handful of women at the same time, go home with them, and have sex in full view of their families, without provoking either anger or jealousy. Some might even like it. We also believed Western men weren't jealous because they ate pork. We believed that a man who ate pork would lack feelings of jealousy and become a cuckold who didn't care whether his mother, sister, or wife had sex with random men.

I am reminded of other disastrous stereotypes repeated among our people back there—that once someone reached Europe, they entered paradise through its widest gates. Europe was portrayed as permanent unemployment. Money flowed to you without account or accountability, and wealth was gathered in record time. Not to mention stereotypes of how citizenship was granted immediately and that, once it was, you could then practice a form of colonialism against the country, its sons, and especially its daughters.

There were those who excavated the legacy of colonialism and tried to use it for themselves, exhuming history and its bloody accretions, excuses that enabled them to practice obscenity as though taking revenge for their supposed ancestors. Their illusions developed to such an extent that they imagined a historic revenge. They foolishly saw themselves as unique, "and in Al-Qisas there is a saving of life for you, O people of understanding, that you may become righteous." They imagined this new life as a new paradise, and that by punishing the country's women and children, they were avenging and commemorating their predecessors.

There were others who lived here in body, while their spirits were eager to stay over there. They went on living inside that dark history, and the darkness of those miserable men of religion who passed their dirty fatwas against those different from them, using up their money and their blood. You would find these men thrilled when the country where they lived, or a neighboring one, was struck by a terrorist attack. Their stupidity might even lead them to describe these terrorist events as God fulfilling his promise to his Muslim followers and punishing those who deviated from the straight and narrow.

And there were those who had another miserable thought: they belonged to a category of survivors to whom God would give power, dominion, and influence, and who would be feared and dreaded. He would become a leader, would rule the land of infidels and achieve new conquests in the twenty-first century, returning Islam to splendor, glamour, and power.

In this way, some Muslims in the West experienced blatant contradictions. You could see them withdraw into themselves. They kept their old flimsy clothes, keen to appear out of place and time, as people who could not adapt to the details of their new life but yearned to keep the rights, money, and aid they got from those they hated—from the donors who protected them. It is a crazy feeling that leaves a person blind and dumb.

Now, back to the British man's question about choosing between bad and worse, where one choice is hostile to a country while the other is hostile to all of humanity. Back to this man's attempt to keep me in the category of the accused, one who is obliged to produce answers that remove him from the prison of accusations in which he is jailed.

It was futile to explain that there were other ways besides the two to which he restricted me—how terrorism feeds terrorism and resonates with it, whether hidden by a loose cloak of chauvinism or disguised by the hypocritical and false masks of religion. Or how the revolution called for establishing a free and decent democratic society, which was alien to the monstrous regime that had destroyed the country for decades, plundering its wealth, preventing any potential revival, and killing tens of thousands in ongoing wars against its people while throwing tens of thousands into prisons. Then that same regime claimed to protect the country from protestors chanting slogans of freedom and dignity, turning peaceful protests into violent clashes with the military and with groups the president himself armed and sent out, allegedly to confront and fight terrorism. This, from the creator and exporter of terrorism to the rest of the world. He who kills a person kills all of humanity.

I felt pity for the person who had asked me that question. He, too, was a victim of stereotypes, much like the ones that were a heavy and destructive burden for many of my countrymen, who found themselves in the streets and cities of Europe after being displaced from their destroyed cities in Syria. I didn't consider asking him a similar question, he who was under the illusion that the Assad regime was secular. He believed what the media told him, that the regime was defending the state. The news rewrites events according to their political biases and agendas, those known and implied. The perpetrator is transformed into a victim and the victim is remade as executioner.

I have no interest in choosing a method of murder. What concerns me is choosing a way to live, a method of humanitarian living that offers many branches. But the warmongers and thugs who rule the world are trying to make people choose between two dead ends, to keep them from hoping for a decent life.

I will not choose how I die, even though I live in a gloomy and deadly world. I will, however, continually search for ways to live, ways to be happy and coexist. I will search for a freedom fit for all people in the East and West, not the partial freedom that tyrants bestow on their oppressed people, as though it is theirs. These people have found themselves hostages of miserable circumstances. They are prisoners in thick shackles that will take a long time to destroy, to finally become free to choose a life away from the terrorism of politicians and the merchants of religion.

A Thorny Issue

My dear Agatha, I remember reading about a discussion you had with some Syrians about religion. You say, in your book, that the topic of religion is "a very vexed question in this particular part of the world, for Syria is full of fiercely fanatical sects of all kinds, each willing to cut each other's throats for the good cause!" I can assure you, in light of the many paradoxes I've encountered and questions I've been asked that were slaps to the face, that hatred is a fire raging in various parts of the world, and it ravages the souls of people everywhere.

I call on you, Dame Agatha, so that I might recount some of the news from your country and our world, which you left. I have imagined so many of the crimes that take place in your novels. A few people have gone so far as to accuse you of teaching those in the criminal profession new techniques to develop their skills, saying that you transformed your characters' lives in order to orchestrate strange crimes, engineering worlds and terrible details to warn your readers of what's on its way.

I am not concerned with interpreting your novels and analyzing your writerly goals and intentions . I do not wonder whether crime novels resonate in the real world because, in fact, they are the world's echo, whether the literature preceded the real world or followed and imitated it. Crime in literature is placed there intentionally, to add color to the broad literary field and to chart a different path, mixing reality with imagination and extracting from the human soul its cruelest and most brutal elements. It conveys made-up scenes from a reality that transcends the limits of imagination by surprising us with strange crimes.

Before the British voted to leave the European Union, various contradictory signs emerged, some of which one might describe as steps on the path to coexistence, others as steps toward aggression and crime.

When Sadiq Khan, a man of Pakistani descent, was elected mayor of the city of London, those advocating to remain in the European Union considered it a big step on the path to remaining in the European Union and thus part of Europe's vast space, its varied colors. But there were those who considered it nothing more than an electoral move that didn't extend beyond the election game and its purposes, both hidden and declared.

The struggle between Brexiteers and Remainers reached its peak when a man killed the Labor party deputy, Jo Cox, on June 16, 2016, in the village of Birstall in northern England. The man, who chanted that Britain came first, later declared his name in court to be "Death to traitors... Freedom to Britain."

Which Britain was this killer imagining, when he called for its liberation? The one drowning in hatred of itself and others, engulfed in the racism that is its scourge? What mad images could possibly have led to this level of horrific and violent hate?

I was deeply saddened and shocked by the news of Jo Cox's death. Although horrific killings, death, and destruction take place daily in my country, we have plunged past shock and despair and into numbness. This death brought me back to a different reality. I am not saying I was divorced from reality, but I thought that this kind of thing was part of Britain's past, which had included bloody periods on the path to establishing its present democracy.

For decades, there were no prisoners of conscience in Britain, but with the killing of Jo Cox, a raucous siren sounded across the land. This country, which had passed laws guaranteeing a person's right to their opinion, now saw the return of a different and more dangerous type of transgression: political assassination. This return would herald new lessons in Britain's contemporary political history.

Many inside and outside Britain had reservations about accusing Cox's killer of being mentally unstable, suffering from psychological disorders. They saw it as a pretext, set forward when the criminal wasn't fair-skinned or a foreigner from beyond the West. Or, more to the point, when the criminal wasn't Muslim or Arab, or a descendant of Muslims or Arabs.

Is there really a plot to demonize Arabs and Muslims in the West and turn them into the Jews of the twenty-first century? To force them to live in ghettos, deport and isolate them in certain places within Europe, and to construct electrified, insulating walls—however invisible—that besiege them and restrict their freedoms and movements?

Such beliefs, akin to conspiracy theories, are foremost in the minds of Arabs, Middle Easterners, and those in neighboring countries. For years, these ways of thinking have accumulated, bringing skepticism and a loss of self-confidence, coupled with a history of Western colonial practices and Western governments' domination of the region and its people, dividing and parceling them out as if they shared an ancestral heritage, and so had inherited a right to sovereignty and leadership of that world.

Some consider Cox an icon of coexistence and peace, others a victim of her bold recklessness in criticizing particular policies and ideas. She thought she could change the world. Her killer assassinated her thoughts along her with her body.

When I think about the meaning of heroism and redemption, of love and hate, I remember some isolated events here and there, details that color the painting of our current era. For whoever is a hero to one people, or to one nation or party, is cursed in the eyes of another.

There is still disagreement among the British people about whether the

Irishman Bobby Sands (1954-1981) was a hero or a criminal. He was arrested by British authorities for his role in the struggle to liberate Ireland from British rule, and he was sentenced to many years in prison. He died in prison on the sixty-sixth day of his hunger strike, at the age of twenty-seven, and left behind a number of writings that were leaked from his cell, in which he spoke of his reality, hopes, dreams, and suffering, and of the oppression of prison and the injustices he suffered.

Sands would look out on the other side of the prison walls and try to imagine what might exist in the space of freedom, but then despair would overcome him once again. He would talk to himself about how, when he looked around at the grave in which he lived, he felt immersed in hell, and that his jailers took the forms of mutilated demons, ready to leap on him at any moment.

Was he a monster disguised as a hero? A hero whose enemies made him into a beast that killed itself when it realized it couldn't kill them first?

Many people were fond of Jo Cox, especially refugees: for her sympathy and advocacy for Syrian refugees, her stance on the war in Syria, and her support for Syrians' right to freedom from tyranny. She was regarded as a model politician who put her humanity above all other interests and considerations. Maybe that was what led her killer to assassinate her humanity along with her body.

Does this mean that we're facing a near future of hatred? Was the British vote to exit the European Union a victory for Cox's killer, or was all this nothing more than coincidence? Will we one day witness the victory of values over political games?

There are exacerbating types of invasive hatred. The paradigm of hatred is: one stranger for another, one refugee for another. The saying that "a stranger to one is a relative to another" has become "a refugee to one is an opponent and rival to another."

One example is the new refugees, now going through circumstances similar to those experienced by previous refugees, and the children of refugees, whether first or second generation, who advocated for Britain to leave the European Union, thinking it would benefit them. They are under the impression that the coast will become clear, so to speak, and that they will benefit from the privileges granted to them as refugees, and later as British citizens, without having to compete with other immigrants and refugees.

Here, the hatred of the other is a sign of self-loathing. It is evidence of myopia and blindness, a sort of victimization of one another where victims become executioners, eliminating the others who share their conditions.

One example of political manipulation and fraud—where politicians deceived both themselves and their constituents, denying the values and principles on which their civilizations are built—is an incident where the classic nude statues in Italy's Capitoline Museum were covered up in 2016, during a visit by Iran's president, Hassan Rouhani. This gratification and acceptance of Iranian delusions resulted in the signing, in the Italian museum, of seventeen million euros' worth of trade deals between the Italian Prime Minister, Matteo Renzi, and the Islamic Republic.

Does this tell you anything, Agatha? How would you classify this act, if placed in the crime literature that you've helped to propagate? Would you consider this incident, where statues were covered up with miserable boxes, an attempt to assassinate history and civilization for the sake of money, agreements, and tempting contracts? Is sweet talk, flattery and deception now used at the expense of distortions to civilization, denying the values of humanity? Could the Iranian president really be offended by a seemingly nude figure, he who has no shame in supporting tyrannical regimes that kill their own people around the world—he who is actively supporting, through Iranian forces, the oppression of the Syrian people? Is he embarrassed by a statue, but not by the killings of thousands of people and the displacement of millions, which are due to his policies and actions? How does one balance right and duty on one hand, while on the other holding dishonor and shame in the black world market with its endless dark allies?

The business of the statues shows a terrible misery for the European, who is apparently quick to lie down for the temptation of gold and the sparkle of money, to the point that he begins to salivate. He is quick to sacrifice the values on which his country's civilization was built for the sake of his Iranian guest's comfort. This was not done to be a good host—no, it was done to lead his guest gradually into his trap, one that he, himself, fell into in the end, harming his own culture and history.

Some might say that interests direct governments and regimes. But does that mean these governments must develop a mob mentality that seeks only to secure those interests? Does this apply to those who describe other governments as gangs, robed in the guise of law while acting to suit their own interests?

I remember that France refused to make a similar gesture during Rouhani's visit to Paris. As a result, France was subjected to terrorist crimes that resulted in the deaths of many innocent people. Is this not an indication of the axis of evil, of which the Iranian regime represents one arm, spreading evil in the world?

Yet hardly any time passes before the media is preoccupied with yet another terrorist attack. The attacks that gain the most coverage occur in Europe or America, and the ones who commit these crimes reflect negatively on thousands of millions of people, who are then criminalized. The refugee becomes a subject of doubt and suspicion, and it's up to him to prove his worthiness or eligibility for innocence. He is an innocent, required to prove his innocence. He is treated as a suspect, a potential terrorist in disguise, a bomb, and no one knows when he might detonate and destroy himself and his surroundings.

The media manipulates the public. They emphasize small incidents and turn them into disastrous events by placing them under a microscope. They overanalyze, break them down and contrast the pieces, then suggest that these are the greatest issues of this or that period, before moving on to feed on another small story. Deceptively, the media charts a line of thinking for people to follow. They define lines of action and propose solutions and ways to approach a subject.

When the global media focused on the image of the drowned child, Alan Kurdi, on the shore of the Aegean Sea, the world sympathized with him. It was a painful picture of a drowned, innocent child, but the pictures of others who also drowned, including Alan's brother, were deemed unworthy of attention and sympathy.

By using such narratives, it is easy to find ways to garner public sympathy and support for the refugee cause, through the image of an innocent child. But the bigger and more important matter—what caused these refugees to flee their countries—is left unexamined, as is any discussion of ways to stop the wars in those countries and thereby to end the disasters that are sure to follow.

The image of the Syrian child Omran, with his blank stare, also shocked the world, and led to the tears of a CNN anchor who said, emotionally, that she had no idea who might have bombed the child's home. Yet all of this served as emotional impact only. The child's image on the front page of the most important international newspapers in no way reduced the damage in Syria at the time.

Images of the hundreds of children who were killed by chemical gases used by the Assad regime in Eastern Ghouta, in Damascus, in Aleppo, and in other areas did not get much attention from the media, unlike the images of Alan and Omran. They both deserve sympathy and attention, yes, but what about all the others who were killed, who no one is interested in photographing? Even if their pictures were shown by the media, they would not carry the desired impact, especially on the Western public, and so they are not displayed in context. Parts of the pictures are edited out, to direct people's attention away from them.

Perhaps these are random incidents in the East and West, but I address them in order to convey to you, Mrs. Christie, scenes from our world after you left it. Perhaps your characters can live amidst the crime that escalates day by day in our modern world. They would enjoy their innocence as imaginary characters who, if they took on realistic roles, would embody less violence than prevails in our present reality.

I won't overanalyze every detail, nor will I issue judgments and accusations here and there, but I do wish to convey some of what I feel, about what happened and is happening, as it directly affects me, my family, and my country, as well as my global family, to which I belong, having left my country. We are a family across borders with an identity that doesn't belong to one place, a culture that surpasses cultures and pains that surpass time, place, and also borders.

In the time that it took me to write this chapter, more acts of terrorism have taken place in London and Manchester. They warn that the bridge of love is melting away like a pile of snow threatened by a raging fire. The flames of hate are eating away at it. There is also a hatred like hot coals beneath ash, burning slowly around me, here in your country that my daughters know as home, and no other home beside it. Even the atheists are muttering, "God help us."

To Become an Outcast

Dear Agatha, did you feel like an outcast when you were traveling around my country decades ago? When you met people, did you see yourself as a pariah in their eyes? Did you translate the madness and oppression and loss that you encountered into the crime imagined in your books, as an outlet for what otherwise could have ignited sparks of hatred toward others?

Perhaps the temporary nature of your presence protected you from ostracism, since you had the option of returning to your country at any time. This is a luxury that most refugees do not have, as they are doomed to live "here" and dream of "there." I have no doubt that the human being is an exotic realm, molded from the contradictions that make up his inner self and keep him walking in a maze, orbiting around himself.

There are often growing feelings of ostracism in refugees who find themselves uprooted, in search of other soil on which to settle for a hopeful future. To be a refugee is to be anxious, an outcast, a hostage of one's own mind, memories, and nostalgia. And no matter how much you try to suppress your feelings and focus on your life's path and the horizon that looms ahead of you—on the urgings of daily life—you will not be free from the power of your inner terror.

I frequently see police patrols moving from one place to another, hear their sirens as they rush in this or that direction, and I find myself overcome with baseless fear. Police cars make me panic because I feel I am being accused of something I have not done.

Perhaps I have not yet overcome my phobia of the Syrian police and intelligence services. There, they are the enemy of the people. It's as if the people who work for them are poisoned with an ideology of hate that makes them see all citizens as criminals who must be caught and punished.

No doubt refugees are anxious people, who feel subconsciously accused, and coincidences play a role in adding to their anxiety and confusion. I once attended a parent-teacher meeting for children who were graduating from kindergarten and moving up to first grade. I chose to sit with my wife at the back of the hall to avoid attracting attention, especially since my English was far more limited than that of the native speakers present. I preferred to follow the discussion without taking part or asking questions.

The chairs laid out in the hall were flimsy, and I winced when I sat on one of them, worried that it wouldn't support my weight. Moments after we were seated, my youngest daughter, Roz, became fidgety and started to cause trouble, drawing people's attention to us. Her sister had left with her teacher and a group of kids whose names had been called. I tried to distract Roz by lifting her up so she could see the stage over people's heads, which calmed her down a bit, but then she demanded to stand on my knees so she could see better. The music was loud, and the kids were all dancing to the beat, so she, too, began to sway and dance as I held her hands and tried to balance her on my knees. Then, suddenly and without warning, the chair crashed beneath me and I found myself sprawled out on the floor.

The sound of the crash was shocking. Everyone's eyes turned to me, and I became embarrassed and confused. I quickly assured people that I was fine, that no harm was done, but I was worried about the stereotypes that Europeans might have when they encounter someone from a Muslim or Middle Eastern background, especially since I have black hair, olive skin, and Middle Eastern features. As I laid there on the floor, I read in people's eyes a great panic at hearing that loud bang, especially since there had been several recent terrorist attacks in London and Manchester. I told myself that a refugee would always be conspicuous, no matter how hard he tried to hide his embarrassment and confusion.

When I read the book *A Fly in the Soup,* by the Yugoslavia-born American writer Charles Simic (Belgrade, b. 1938), I felt as though I were reading a chapter from our present. He writes about the different chapters of his life, especially those related to his experiences with asylum and alienation. Simic points out that their dreams as refugees did not exceed the bounds of their city of Belgrade, and that his family, like many other families, was able to see the world for free thanks to Hitler's wars and Stalin's control of Eastern Europe. He says that they did not cooperate with the Germans, nor were they from the aristocracy, nor were they political exiles. He says they were insignificant and decided nothing for themselves—that everything was arranged for them by world leaders.

I lived in more than one position. As Simic says: "Immigration, exile, being uprooted and made a pariah may be the most effective way yet devised to impress on an individual the arbitrary nature of his or her own existence." I ostracized myself even though I never saw exclusion in people's eyes when they looked at me. I became hypersensitive to every little thing I encountered and interpreted people's spontaneous looks as ones of contempt and skepticism, and I wished to justify the reasons I was among them.

I fully relate to what Simic wrote about his need to justify his presence and how it became clear to him that he would not succeed in the usual ways, which was why he began to write and draw. He didn't know what to do. He mentioned that his past life taught him that planning for the future was a waste of time, and that his father used to jokingly ask, "Where are you going to migrate next?" He wrote sorrowfully that the experience of exile in the twentieth century had not yet ended, that "people like him and me were its laboratory animals. Strangest of all, one of the rats was writing poetry."

The urge some Syrians feel to justify their presence in Europe has surpassed the mere need to convince themselves and reached a need to convince others. Asylum has become a mask they wear to hide their past shame, the faults and sins they committed in the past, and sometimes the crimes, as though this chapter of asylum could erase people's memories or cause amnesia.

There are those who persist in exaggerating their heroic deeds and previous struggles, as well as the roles they played in various events. Yet they forget the names of those who witnessed these heroic acts, or they remember the witnesses' names but these people have passed away, or they name witnesses who are as unreliable and deceptive as they are. So their behavior becomes less persuasive and more worthy of ridicule, lament, and disgust. They exemplify the popular fable of the fox without a tail.

In my mind, a question persists about how to dispel these feelings of ostracism that reside in the refugee's soul and that occupy his being. I find that time is a panacea for all the pains of asylum, as it enables people to rearrange themselves and rebuild their personalities in a way that combines what they used to be and what they ought to become. And far from being the outcast that the refugee deep down senses himself to be, he can now choose to affiliate with the place where he finds his own humanity and existence, unlike how it was under the regime of murder, terrorism, and criminality.

We expect people to want to relocate to a home-in-exile that makes them feel safe, confident, and relatively reassured, a place where they can be free from feelings of ostracism, panic, suspicion, and fear of all things and people. This is the first step to overcoming the bridge between stability and dispossession, between the wasted self and the dream of peace, security, and happiness that they desire. Anyone who holds himself captive to feelings of hatred cannot be freed from ostracism and aggression, because he will find opposition, rejection, and repulsion in everything he encounters.

At times, I encounter refugees who carry an unjustified grudge against the country that harbors them, embraces them, and grants them what they were denied in those countries that were supposed to be their homelands. What is perhaps yet more surprising and distressing is the gloating attitude they take in some of their writings, when they talk about terrorist attacks in this or that Western country. The irony is that those relishing in the suffering of these countries, implicitly or publicly, actually carry those countries' nationalities. They claim to be overburdened with taxes and write that the people of these countries, who treated them with humanity and respect, should suffer the same horrors they endured in their native countries, so as to taste the same bitterness they had to taste, while sipping from the cup of terrorism that they themselves imported to these countries. They are quick to be hostile, and they do not differentiate between the policies of governments that employ the logic of interest and influence, and innocent people who dream only of safety and a free and decent life.

It is no secret that such gloating eyes will ultimately fixate on their owners, the same people who live on aid given by the countries they oppose. They remain perpetual outcasts in their own eyes, and in the eyes of others, because they like to be in a state of ostracism and oppression, forever biting the hands that pulled them out of the quagmire of loss, and that shelter and provide them with the means of a decent life. They betray themselves in their miserable loyalty to their sick imaginations and deep-rooted hatreds.

TheStrangers' Daughter in Law

Your love for homelands is an obvious weakness
So leave and find replacements for your family and home elsewhere
And the running water will remain clear
And time will not stop.

Lamia Ibn al-Wardi – Omar bin al-Mazfar, Ibn al-Wardi

There's a Kurdish saying that goes: "Xwezî ez bûka xerîba bama û min pesnê mala bavê xwe daba." Roughly translated, it means: "I wish I were the daughter-in-law of strangers, praising my father's family." It refers to people who brag about things that are untrue or that have never taken place. They invent things to puff themselves up, even if they are misleading, a mere delusion. When it comes to the person who leaves his family and home and country, he might claim to be the son of a wealthy and important family, or that he is the mainstay of his family and the center of attention, the focal point in any situation. He might say such things because he considers himself worthy of a sort of importance that he cannot attain in reality. His ability to invent a glorious past for himself is God's way of making up for his current reality, and it gives him a hopeful future to look toward.

Perhaps this example can be applied to many refugees in countries of asylum. I often encounter people from different cities who invoke a glorious past for themselves, creating delusions of their former greatness and cursing the treacherous times that manipulated them and took away their wealth and glory, times that threw them in exile to forever ruminate on their sorrows and remember their glories, which help preserve their grandeur in their minds.

Some speak of the many businesses and factories they used to own in more than one field, while others remember the palaces they lived in and their families' possessions, which they inherited but were lost in the war, and how they "belong to a nation reduced to disgrace." Others create myths about their past, their riches, and their heroisms, and of how they had to leave everything behind to go into exile. This sort expects people to believe everything they say, and, if people don't believe them, they attack other people's histories as forged.

One does not need to hear the boasting glories of a past that existed only in the dreams of its owner and in their imagination. Their reality is a much clearer reflection of their truth than anything they can fabricate, and that has nothing to do with their situation, but with the way they think, for they carry their minds as a burden and a sin from which they cannot be freed. So they create new, innovative stories and fabrications that they impose on their past selves, and they take advantage of people's ignorance and inability to go to their homelands to discover their true past and false glory.

One loses his self-respect and appreciation when he searches for them in a sea of misinformation, delusions, and lies. And no matter how much a person speaks of his past glory, his way of thinking and acting will expose him and reveal his truth, for it is the mirror of his reality and true self. This reminds me of the poet, Ibn al-Wardi, who said, "Never state my origin and faction. / Rather, the 'origin' of a youth is that which he attains." The saying points to more than one meaning, and I would like to imagine that human transcendence is the most important of all these, as the person himself takes precedence over any achievement.

Is a refugee "the daughter-in-law of strangers" who boasts about the inheritance of her family, which does not exist, while she stands exposed to her surroundings, especially her husband's family, who sees her reality because her actions expose her true self? One does not need tales of the greatness of their family, for greatness manifests itself in behavior, not in allegations.

Some refugees try to remove themselves from the category of refugee. They place themselves in the ranks of exiled princes and kings, who seek to return home and rebuild their lost kingdoms, to restore their past glories. In the meantime, they are wasting their present and future by not equipping themselves or fighting for a decent living. And a decent living does not mean making money—it means building a life of work and value, expanding the circle of communication and influence, striving to achieve success in the various fields they engage in or seek to enter. It means building a solid and realistic foundation for a life away from lies, and events both forged and imagined.

It is no secret that a refugee's relationship with his new home, if he has come from a miserable cultural and intellectual background, does not guarantee his integration with his surroundings. Rather, it makes him hostile towards himself and his new world. There are incidents that might incite the stranger to sabotage his surroundings, for as the saying goes, "If a country is not yours, shit in the middle of the road and walk away." This saying stems from the accumulation of unjustified hatred for new places, which become new homelands for strangers. This historical cultural incitement to tamper with the safety of a place, and disturb the comfort of its people, raises both questions and distaste.

On the other hand, perhaps the army mentality applies to the refugee's world, where the reward is granted to the individual, but the punishment is collective. For if a refugee achieves something or performs a remarkable act, he is rewarded for his achievement or distinction. But if a refugee commits a mistake or errs or does something bad, then the whole group feels the punishment. This way, the group rejects the offender who is causing them trouble and disturbing their comfort, so they isolate him or prevent him from committing a wrong in order to protect themselves from possible penalties.

In the country of asylum, this method is applied in reward and punishment, and while the penalties are not directly imposed by authoritative and angry groups, they are imposed in a modern way that corresponds to the composition and structure of society. After all, ostracism and contempt are among the unspoken tools of punishment. If a refugee commits a crime, it causes embarrassment to his whole group. So classification becomes a way to identify and subsequently pass judgment or apply restrictions and limits.

For example, the former British Prime Minister, David Cameron, once appeared on British and international media saying that a small percentage of Syrians were sympathetic to ISIS and other Islamic extremist groups. His statement triggered the wrath of many, but in reality, it is necessary to confront the self and state, for in fact these terrorist organizations are the product of a terrorist life, and a mixture of subjective and objective reasons came to form them and launch them into the world.

This small percentage he spoke of is the most difficult to classify, for it is possible for anyone to belong to that percentage. So one has to oppose that percentage. But if you go overboard in your show of opposition, then the tables will turn, and you will draw attention to yourself. In that instance, you will be expected to prove that you are not merely playing the role of a peaceful refugee while you wait for the opportunity to commit a crime that you subconsciously desire to plan and execute.

If a refugee achieves distinction in a field, this is due to the conditions created for him by the country that embraced and nurtured him, thus guaranteeing his distinction and success. But if a refugee commits a wrongdoing, it is the fault of his previous country and the culture that raised him and set him loose to become a danger to everyone. He then negatively impacts others, who are also judged for his actions. Blunt is the blade of the guillotine of oral and prejudicial provisions.

In countries that have reached advanced levels of privacy and independence, iniquity is generalized by referring to a person's social and cultural background, as well as their ethnic, religious, and geographical affiliations. This generalization contradicts the values claimed by society in a blatant manifestation of the contradiction that, in turn, contributes to shaping a new reality.

If the accused is said to be innocent until proven guilty, then the opposite is true for refugees, who are guilty until proven innocent. As for how they are accused, this is another matter, which manifests in many different ways.

It seems that the military's methods don't work as well when applied to civil society. Nowadays, a person is rewarded individually for his accomplishments, while he is placed in a circle of accusations with others who share the nationality, religion, or appearance of people who have committed a crime. Thus he becomes, in the eyes of those around him, guilty until proven innocent. But he is met with doubt if he tries to defend himself in the face of these accusations.

The Logic of Letting Go

A person's accumulated experiences contribute to the creation of their convictions. A person might change from one situation to the next, but each experience will add to their knowledge and further ground them. New experiences also reveal aspects of life a person would not otherwise have been aware of, had they not been forced to go through them. Life remains a school of experimentation, where lessons are taught and wisdom is shared.

Some people believe it best not to throw anything away, no matter how small or insignificant, even if it is of no value or feasibility, because they might end up needing it. Such logic was common in our town when I was young. My grandmother held onto many things that she always said we needed, and she never threw anything away that she thought she might use one day.

Perhaps my mother's logic was also the result of accumulated days and experiences, for she had been through a lot in her life. She moved around with my grandfather, who married her in secret and took her to his village, and from there to Amuda. A life of poverty, transience, and homelessness taught my grandmother that the simplest things can be costly, and she might need just about anything one day. She kept many pots in her small mud house that she thought she would come to need in the future.

I don't know how my grandfather managed to persuade my grandmother to run away with him when he was already married and a father of four children, the eldest of whom was almost as old as my grandmother. My grandmother would tell me a different story of how she married my grandfather every time I asked about it. She would also forget what she had told me before, and, when I reminded her, she would accuse me of making up events and stories that never happened. She would tell me that the books I read spoiled my mind. Then she would laugh loudly, close her eyes, and smile as she lamented how I had turned out.

My grandmother had herself been a mother of two children, a boy and a girl, when she ran away with my grandfather in the late forties. I would always admonish her for leaving her two children behind to be raised by relatives and strangers so she could follow lust and instinct, running away with my grandfather, who had spun sweet words and promises about how he would give her a nice, comfortable life. Instead, he became a burden on her in their final years together, and then he passed away, leaving her a middle-aged woman to raise their seven children alone, the eldest of whom was my father, who continued to take care of his younger siblings, even after he married my mother. He managed to take care of two families during a time when work, education, comfort, and security were scarce.

My grandmother Noufa was unable to meet her daughter because she died during childbirth. She excused marrying her off to a relative in their village at a young age by saying she would be kept under the watchful eye of family, protected from strangers and vagabonds like my grandfather, who had deceived my grandmother and persuaded her to run away with him.

At the time, people said that orphans were brought up like animals, with no manners or education, and so it was best to protect them from the evils of real life. They married the girls off at a young age and tried to restrict the boys, keeping them busy with work like herding, farming, and physical labor. They would be pressed to marry a relative who had a fault of some kind or lacked beauty.

My grandmother also did not meet her son, who she left in the village of

Kurashiki, located on the Turkish side of the border north of the train line, which forms a border between north and south. For us, it was a historical as well as geographical separation of family and relatives, north and south. After nearly half a century, her son became a grandfather, and he looked a lot like my father. Life had not been kind to him, but he became a skilled hunter who roamed the mountainous areas that surrounded his home. He went on hunting trips alone, camped out alone with his rifle and nets, and lived in the wilderness, where he survived off what he hunted. He was the most famous hawk hunter in the area, but he was also known for his skill in hunting deer, rabbits, and foxes.

This may have been his way of compensating for his marginalization in the village where he lived his entire life, since he was stigmatized by the shame of his mother's abandonment of him and his little sister. Perhaps he was trying to prove that he could be better than everyone else in the village, and perhaps hunting gave him pleasure: capturing creatures that tried to escape him.

When I met him, he was a dignified man of few words. His rough hands pointed to hardships that he had endured while bearing the burdens of orphanhood and loneliness. For, in addition to being a famous hunter, he was known as the best builder in the region, called on by both the wealthy and the poor. I don't know if this made up for him not being able to build a luxurious home for himself and his family, or if it made up for his inability to restore his previous life and patch up the ruin his mother had left behind by running away and abandoning him and his sister.

I often wonder about the logic behind my grandmother's hoarding so many trivial things. Was it her way of compensating for abandoning her children? Or maybe she did not want, ever again, to neglect something she had, no matter how meaningless the object. Had she learned a lesson about the logic of abandonment after applying it in her own life with neither awareness nor planning, and then become obsessed with the need to obtain, own, and keep things?

Many stories have been told about my grandfather. Some were mere myths with supposed superheroes, and these became part of my memories of early childhood. I remember that he kept a gun close at hand, although he spent the last years of his life unable to walk and needed help to move. But he was convinced that someone was going to break in to arrest him or take revenge.

It was a common practice in Kurdish tribes to kill the daughter who ran away from home along with the man who took her. This may have played a role in my grandfather's paranoia and the ultimate ruin of his life. I remember him placing his gun in my hand and teasing my grandmother, who would admonish him for being a dangerous influence on me at such a young age. I never heard my grandfather's gun go off, but I'm sure its proximity made him feel safe, even when he was on his deathbed.

My grandmother used to say that my great-grandfather escaped a death sentence during the war, although she often confused WWI and WWII. She would say that he was moved to a remote prison and so he bribed a jailer he knew, then took three guns with him and fled to live for months in the mountain wilderness as part of his escape to his village.

She would drift off into her imaginary tales, telling me how he avoided coming face to face with bears in the cold mountains, but that he was sometimes forced to shoot them and grill their flesh for food. She would look so happy as she spoke of how he walked for days alone, while at night he was accompanied by two invisible guards. She would then wink at me, insinuating that he was a descendant of an honest and righteous family, and that I had a great-grandfather who'd lived among deer in the wilderness, who fed and cared for him as he worshiped God in the caves and grottos, away from human influence.

My father would stamp his feet on the ground near where he sat, confirming that he indeed had a grandfather who was imprisoned by the Ottomans, and that one day when they released the prisoners in the courtyard for a break, a strong wind suddenly came and carried him off, away from the prison and the reach of the guards, and he was able to escape his death sentence.

It is not a matter of inventing delusional heroics, but rather a compulsion to cling to imaginative myths and recount them as facts that must be believed, as though they had occurred in real life. For confirmation, there were the many witnesses who believed this miracle and treated my great-grandfather, Darwish, as a favored and pious man. The tale's concluding words, which were the secret that silenced all skeptics, including myself, were that God places his secrets in his weakest creations, and that the saints of God are usually hidden in the garments of the poor and the dervishes.

How has the logic behind letting things go—and its opposite, hoarding them—affected the different stages of my life?

I kept to that logic for a time, clinging to a lot of small things, like a piece of paper or a simple souvenir, keeping them in a private locker. I kept a lot of exciting things that I would tell myself I must never waste.

But each time I start a new chapter of my life, I also let go of some of the things from the previous chapter. At times, I laugh at my past concerns about things that I later realize are so small and insignificant. But some things do move on with me to the next stage. They withstand the rigorous process of classification and organization, and they appear timeless and relevant to all life's stages.

Can a person be stripped of his memory by removing the details, things, and places that make up his memories and link them in a cumulative way? Can one's memory keep all these details? Are the things that accumulate in a person's reservoir of reality or memory the salt of his times and places?

When I moved from one room to another in the same house, I reviewed and rearranged the things I owned, my books and souvenirs. I went through them and disposed of many, and felt as though my mind, in turn, was reducing its load and inheritance. And when I got married and moved into my own home, I placed some of these souvenirs in a box that I kept at my parents' house. Later, when I moved from Amuda to Damascus, I disposed of yet more things, along with books that I found more suited to the earlier stages of my life.

I don't believe that all the books we acquire, or that are given to us, deserve to occupy a permanent place in our library. Books are like friends, and just as there is a friend for a certain road or a journey, and a lifelong friend who crosses all of life's chapters with you, there are also books suitable for a certain temporary experience, books you can rely on during your travels, that can fill time on a journey. Such a book may journey on with you and become part of your bookshelf, or you may abandon it at the nearest station. And there are the books of a lifetime, and these books transcend time and space. You will need them from time to time, as they fill a mental or spiritual void created by a trauma or caused by a setback in your life, and you will find these books waiting for you, to restore your balance. These books are as rare as true friends.

It is also said that the three impossibilities—the ghoul, the phoenix, and the loyal friend—are possible in the world of books. For loyalty to the library that has founded one's memory is rare in the sea of regeneration and overflowing human creativity. One may return to the books in his library only to find them too simple and fragile. A person's awareness, consciousness, and empathy may have changed him over time so that he finds himself yet again disposing of his books at the nearest station.

I was forced once, under the weight of the war and intensifying battles and after a series of intermittent nighttime clashes, to leave my house in the town of Shebaa, which was in the countryside outside Damascus. I had moved in only a month and a half earlier. I quickly grabbed my laptop, our passports and official identification documents, university degrees, and very little clothing before I rushed out of the house. I left everything else in place. But before I walked out the door, I took a few pictures of the house, because I had a feeling, almost a certainty, that I would never return there, that I would never see that house again and that everything I left behind would be lost. That abandonment was very difficult for me.

I regret not grabbing my photo album, or the tape of my engagement and wedding party, or some of my books and films. I left the household furniture and the foundation of my memories there. Here, I am trying to refurnish my mind with old memories using the game of recovery, acquisition, and abandonment.

One may become prisoner to a logic that he has not chosen for himself, but by which he is still bound. Thus, the logic of letting go becomes something I return to in every stage of my life. When I left Sharjah, for example, I left a small library behind, along with souvenirs and other objects. I made sure that my load walking out did not exceed a large bag, and books took up too much space. I needed to tuck away clothes and necessities. Later, in Beirut, I gave away books and clothes to friends because I had acquired new ones. I had to sift through them so I could keep the most important ones and lighten my load. I did the same thing in Egypt. When I left Cairo, I found myself forced to give up a lot of what I had, for I had collected too many books and things to carry on my journey. My wife and only daughter at the time had followed me to Cairo, so our luggage became heavier and more difficult to manage.

Letting things go becomes a habit with the passage of time, and with the succession and accumulation of experience. I was worried that I would soon begin to abandon my friends the way I have abandoned my things, but

I quickly overcame that fear. I overcame it automatically because I found myself forced to plunge into the fields of memory, recovering the details of events that I had gone through, crystallizing my identity and memory and paving my life in books and in reality.

When a hoarder does not arrange the things he considers precious to him, then they become a source of loss and confusion. He might blame his chaotic lifestyle for his confusion, and, when he moves on with his life, he might feel a sense of disorientation following the loss of his arranged chaos. A person who regrets disposing of his things will continue to ring his conscience from time to time until he succeeds in finding a path that relieves him of the whispers in his mind and convinces him of the need to let go of his illusions.

I admit that, after I immigrated from my homeland, I lost the desire to speak. I preferred privacy and isolation. I avoided calling many of my friends who I am sure believed that immigration had changed me or my situation—as, indeed, it had helped me achieve partial success in the world of writing and publishing—which, in turn, changed my personality and made me deny my old friendships. I don't want to spend time dispelling such doubts and opinions. I am not saying that I am unaffected by their opinions, but rather I admit that I have lost my ability to communicate, despite the availability of social media and my friends' presence and proximity via the world of technology. I have tried many times and failed to regain that ability to converse with no apparent purpose, to invent topics and seek out points of interest and shared experiences.

I feel myself growing more and more solitary as time progresses. I prefer solitude to socializing. I enjoy my loneliness and isolation, the world of books and touring the fields of reading and writing, although this is not possible in reality. For there are responsibilities one must attend to: the household, family, and children.

I am sure that having my family by my side has kept me from sliding into the swamps of despair and loss. I am able to get up every morning, spend time with my daughters Heve and Roz, and embark on new adventures. I am certain that life is worth living because they are part of it, for they make up my entire being.

I often repeat that the greatest outcome of marriage is children. If it were not for the children, life would be a closed cycle of marital insanity, where wife and husband ultimately become enemies. Parenting has restored my belief in life itself and in the world I live in. I have often felt disappointment, being away from them. I felt despair, brokenness, and devastation, but their current presence with me has restored my confidence and faith in myself and others—that there is certainly someone worth living for, clinging to, and being proud of.

Family Mines

Children bear the cost of their parents' and grandparents' sins. They inherit prejudices, collecting them from their mothers and fathers until they become facts and postulates that can neither be questioned nor debated.

I didn't have a chance to see my second daughter, Roz, until she arrived in Edinburgh with my wife, Nisreen, and my oldest daughter, Heve. I had left my pregnant wife with my daughter in Turkey, hoping that the reunion would come quickly, but reality was shocking and harsh.

At the Edinburgh airport, Heve ran toward me and Roz followed her, as younger sisters tend to emulate their older siblings. I didn't cry then. Joy can make one cry, as is well-known, but my tears refused to fall. I was torn up inside for not having been with my wife when she gave birth to our youngest daughter, who I couldn't embrace until she was nearly two years old and had started walking and talking.

Between children and grandparents, memories travel and paths scatter.

Distance carves tunnels into our souls that are impossible to fill, and reunion brings apprehension for what might follow. Far from the poetics imagined on paper, reality is filled with boring and desperate reunions. But any reunion has its charms.

What I remember of my grandfather is a crippled old man who could not finish a sentence without his voice trembling, his throat drying, and his powers failing him. But the stories others have told me of him, and the results of his past actions, contradict my memory.

My grandfather went to the city of Amuda in the thirties after leaving his village, Qasra Qalendra, near Mardin in Turkey. He chose to stay on the outskirts of the city so he could enjoy watching the Mardin lights at night. He insisted that his stay was temporary, and that he would soon return to his village. But the borders of the countries in the region were drawn at the time, and the French and English colonists gradually withdrew from the area, leaving it to later burn down.

"The second wife is always difficult," both my grandmothers often said. The obvious differences between the two women were evident to everyone, and they were reflected in their children as well.

My grandfather married two women, the second of which was my grandmother, who he kidnapped because her family refused to let her marry him, since he was already a married man with four sons. As for his first wife, who was called Nioula, she caught my grandfather's attention when he was visiting her village, which was near Mardin. She was fetching water from the well when the moon reflected off her visage and made her face sparkle and shine, and so my grandfather mistakenly thought her skin was pale and clear. The standard of female beauty for most men in our region is someone pale and blonde. As for the brown and dark-skinned women, they only receive a small amount of attention. He asked the women who were with her at the well, and they told him where she lived. The very next day, he went to her parents' house and asked for her hand in marriage. Indeed, he got what he wanted, as her family approved their marriage. He was extremely happy, as any groom would be. He was not able to see her in the days before their marriage because he was busy furnishing their house. The promised day came, and he got to her village in the afternoon, riding his horse and wearing his best clothes, accompanied by a group of horsemen.

His bride was wearing a veil, which covered her face, which he did not remove because he wanted—he told himself—to take off all her clothes at once that night. So he postponed taking off her veil and took pleasure instead in giving his bride a wedding that her village would speak of for years to come. He didn't remove her veil when they arrived at his village that night, either, despite the villagers' insistence that he do so, and the evening was so beautiful that it obscured her very dark skin. Her face looked bright at night, cheerful and shyly smiling. A grin or laugh in such a situation was considered inappropriate, for the bride must not look eager to be married, or else people would think her desperate or happy to be rid of her family. A big smile would invite gossip that people in the village would spread, promote, and invent.

The night passed, and it was an ideal wedding night. It was in the morning, when the newlyweds woke at noon, that the drama began. My grandfather was shocked and grieved by her very brown face, since he had seen her only once before then at night. His look of disgust made her despise him immediately. My grandfather swore to take a second wife, and she swore to make his life miserable.

She was so dark that people called her "negro, blue, navy" well into her eighties. Such labels, which often upset her, became a stigma forever engraved on her, and they greatly impacted her life.

My grandfather had four children with her, but he kept his oath to marry another, as Islam would allow and make halal for him. He was searching for a woman who looked entirely different from his wife when he saw my grandmother, by chance, in the neighboring village. She looked like the opposite of his wife, with blonde hair and pale skin that she had inherited from her Armenian mother. My grandfather was completely taken by her and her golden hair, so he tried everything to win her, but her parents opposed their union. He tried in other ways to convince her of his love and adoration, and she fell for his words and ran away with him.

Now, where does the real disaster lie?

My grandfather used to call his first wife shameful names that referred to her dark skin, and he would withhold money from her, so she became extra careful with the little he did give her. This in turn caused everyone in the village to think she was stingy. She became known as the stingy black woman. I guess the poor woman had never heard of the saying about the Arab man who told his lover, "And they call you a black African / But it's the blackness of musk that makes it so expensive." This served to make her more bitter and hostile towards others, because all she saw in most of them was mockery. She had no defense mechanisms other than her despair and surrender, in the hopes that those around her would eventually stop. She isolated herself in her home and used harsh words and hostility as shields when confronted with a difficult situation. This was reflected in her children, who also retreated from others and became isolated.

The cruelty toward her blackness remains as effective today as it was back then. For, twenty years after her death, to hurt her dark-skinned children or grandchildren, they are compared to their grandmother and assumed to be stingy, as she was. Skin color here is used as an indicator of character, and she is used as a reference. Past judgments remain final. Everyone forgets the mistreatment she faced and focuses only on what came of it. They judge the outcome without weighing the reasons that led to it.

This behavior created walls that no one in the family could transcend. These barriers remained electrified, mined, and clearly visible, despite their apparent invisibility. Racism has affected three generations of the family so far, and remains vivid in memories, often repeated and experienced, again and again. I do not deny the happiness of my late grandmother, Nawfa, when my grandfather told her that her fellow wife was the black, stingy wife, while she was the beautiful and generous blonde.

Even death could not erase that deadly desire for eradication, for revenge.

My grandfather, who stayed relatively close to his village but moved to the other side of the border hoping to one day return, passed away without fulfilling that wish. Today, his grandchildren have adopted that long estrangement. Although now they are spread out all over the world, they imagine a return to their grandfather's estranged home, which has now become theirs. They seized their right to exist and live there and kept their share of his home for themselves. Today's shelters will become tomorrow's homelands for our children and grandchildren. It seems that the wheel of alienation is constantly rolling.

The Murderer is Me

Dear Agatha,

I remember that, in one of the tales you told about the men who worked with your husband, you mentioned a Kurdish woman who left her mud hut to berate her husband for letting the donkey escape his leash. You described how the Kurdish man sighed sadly in response, asking, "Who would want to be a Kurdish husband?" You added, "There is a saying that if an Arab robs you, he will beat you but leave you to live, but if a Kurd robs you he will kill you just for the pleasure of it!"

I don't know where you got this saying, that a Kurd will kill just for pleasure, because it's a generalization about criminality and sin that doesn't fit the logic of a crime novelist. Criminality has no relation to race or identity, but rather is a human condition present at all times and places, and for all peoples and ethnicities in some proportion.

As for what you wrote about the mice, I have had the same experience in your country. Your first night in the city of Amuda was one you said you would never forget as long as you lived. That "No sooner have the lamps been extinguished than mice in their scores—I really believe in their hundreds—emerge from the holes in the walls and the floor. They run gaily over our bed, squeaking as they run. Mice across one's face, mice tweaking your hair—mice! mice! MICE!" I assure you that I will not forget the many nights I spent, in more than one house here in your country, where the mice were walking and having fun, as though reenacting the same experience you had in my city, as if this were some kind of payback. I remember how a friend of mine in London put it: "London is the city of rats."

Which method of killing will you choose?

This time, I address the question to myself, as I sit alone, recollecting the past. When I was exiled from my city of Amuda to a remote village about eighty kilometers away, I had to drive a motorcycle I bought for the journey, because public transport would not reach that village. At least, I would have needed several hours to reach it by public transit, and that was not possible, since my wife was home alone at the time, and my family had migrated to Damascus. At the time, I intended to move to Damascus, and I had submitted requests for relocation to the Ministry of Education, which kept refusing them due to security recommendations.

How can I get that time back? Can I imagine myself a murderer?

It seems that one's willingness to kill is instinctive, and it grows when there are convincing pretexts, something that would justify the attempt to end another person's life.

There was a young man in my town, a violent alcoholic and drug addict who would harass girls. Nobody cared for him, and he went out into the street nearly naked, insulting and yelling at everyone, including his own parents and brothers and sisters. He worshipped his motorcycle, in which he saw himself reflected, so he flaunted it around town, leaving a cloud of dust wherever he drove, honking his annoying horn and blasting his radio.

One day, I had gotten home late, as usual, from the village—the exile. It was late afternoon. My wife was waiting for my return and kept anxiously watching for my arrival, going out to the street now and again, expecting me whenever she heard a scooter. She told me she was surprised by the large number of scooters in our neighborhood, which people used as their main means of transportation. She said she would not have noticed them if I myself had not got one.

After taking a short nap, we went out to walk in the fields. That spring was hopeful and optimistic, and my wife was often alone for long periods, waiting for me. She liked the plains of Amuda and the springtime air in the wheat and cotton fields, and we walked, then limped, to my sister's house on the western side of town. We visited for a while before we walked back home. This was almost our daily routine.

I had noticed the young addict, since he'd crossed our path more than once, hurling vile looks our way. He looked as though he meant us harm. He would speed past us to block the road ahead, or he'd slow his motorcycle down and trail us while blasting his radio. I wouldn't have paid much attention to his behavior if my wife hadn't been with me, and if he hadn't clearly meant to start a fight and hurt us. I almost confronted him, almost stepped in to fight and physically harm him in order to stop his ugly behavior. But he was famous for always wearing a belt with two protruding blades, which he would use like a sword, and he didn't hesitate to threaten or hurt people with it.

I remembered the proverb, that a barking dog seldom bites, but I couldn't trust that this addict and drunkard would be able to control his behavior. Nor was I confident I could control my temper.

My wife told me that he often harassed her. His state of delirious drunkenness made her both pity and fear him. She warned me not to do anything, because he was crazy, and she went on to say that she'd only told me about him so I would be careful.

I was livid, but I got ahold of myself until we reached my sister's house, where various murder plans began to flood my imagination. I imagined ways I could kill him, how I would do it without raising suspicion, how I could make it look like an accident or a natural death. Or else I could make it look like the result of a fight between two drunks or addicts, nothing more.

Could I become a murderer this easily? Could I kill a person who didn't know what he was doing, because he was under the influence of alcohol and drugs? Was there a hidden killer inside me that I kept in a dark corner, that I could bring out at any moment?

Thoughts seized me. I cursed myself, my way of thinking, and how easily a person could plot a murder in the heat of the moment. Then I decided it was better leave him to his fate and do nothing.

Life seems to take revenge in its own way. About a year and a half after that incident, I had left Syria. I phoned my family, and they told me the addict had died, horribly, in a gruesome accident.

In my culture, whenever someone dies, people must pray for the deceased's mercy and eternal rest, no matter who he is. The logic behind this is that mercy is given by God and is not something we humans decide. If the deceased was disliked or hated, then people can celebrate the news of his death inwardly, but they are prohibited from expressing it aloud, saying things like, "He had it coming," or, "His fate fit him," or that his death was inevitable, a punishment for his dirty deeds and the people he had hurt.

I am not saying I was happy or sad to hear of this man's death. Rather, I paused for a while and remembered my plans to murder him, about which I had told no one. It never occurred to me to torture him, in the horrible way he had been tortured at the end. After all, I am repulsed by the sight of violence and blood. I realized that the decisions of life, nature, and destiny outweigh our own plans.

I do not claim tolerance, nor did I wish him mercy. Instead, I find myself talking about the crimes that many people commit against one another, and how they turn the lives of many into a living hell without any repercussions. Or, other times, how punishment takes such a long time to be delivered that you begin to think the criminal succeeded in getting away with it. I tell myself these lessons.

It seems that spontaneous criminals are produced naturally—these are ordinary people who have no desire to commit any crime, but they live in a country where the law is absent, which favors the professional criminals, who ruin people's lives but reassure them enough to keep them in the quagmires of ignorance, backwardness, revenge, and exaggerated, unimportant conflicts. Violence against others is a tool of systemic corruption, such that every person thinks of killing in order to save himself from the crimes being attempted against him, or committed against him and his family.

This ability to kill still keeps me awake, and from time to time it depresses me. I blame myself for thinking about ending the life of another person, regardless of the harm they caused me, and for how they had driven my wife and I to live part of our lives in suspicion and worry.

How could a simple and seemingly normal person be transformed into a killer? Are killers made, or are they running rampant, living amongst us without our knowledge? Does every person carry the will to kill hidden inside them, which might surface under certain circumstances?

The motives, excuses, and justifications for killing plunge us into the reality of bloody violence. Killing has become part of daily life in our region, which is infested with tyranny, wars, madness, and disasters. There is a saying: "Whoever blames the killers and the murdered must try to live in the same conditions ." Yet if they were to preach, on the other hand, about the necessity of killing to survive, it's important to emphasize patience and not to be drawn to the desire for murder and revenge. It's important to avoid all confrontations that could lead to violence and possible crime.

I cannot imagine myself as a writer turned killer, spending years of my life behind bars, lost and forgotten, because of the stupidity of a mad drunk who decided to harass a woman he encountered.

Should I settle this score with him as I remember these events, and curse him both secretly and publicly? Should I invent on paper another way to kill him and thus detail his ending? Doesn't a writer take revenge in his own way, practicing his intent to kill with words when he needs to, while under the weight of hatred?

There is no justification for violence and murder. But there are also what some see as benefits and obligations. There are events that make you confused and stunned by the frivolity of reality, the violence of authority and its tools, who are emptied of any logic as they attempt to fulfill the orders of those in power, adapting to the conditions of its bloody and violent continuation.

But which path would you choose when presented with two options: kill or be killed?

In a certain light, both options appear to be suicide. To kill the other means drowning yourself in a bottomless swamp of blood and brutality that you can escape only by taking your own life. Likewise, choosing to be killed is just another suicide, only more miserable, because you have the desire to live. To choose neither is to live through tragic circumstances, always waiting for the killers to pounce and kill you. After that, to ridicule you and show off your corpse as a trophy. They will make monsters of your family and friends, as well as others who share and advocate for your beliefs.

These are questions that plague me, and I recall something that will never leave my memory and imagination:

When I was displaced from the Damascus countryside in June of 2012, to the city of Amuda, I participated in one of the many protests that the townspeople had organized from the start of the revolution, which had taken on a new form of fraternal confrontation. Certain Kurdish areas were being taken over and released, shifting between a government security agency and the Kurdish Workers' Party, through their Syrian branch: the Democratic Union Party. A man from the city of Homs took part in these exchanges. By then, Homs had suffered greatly from the scourge of war, the siege, the bombings, and destruction. At the protest, people shared parts of his story, and he responded to questions about militarism and resistance to the security gangs and violent militias who served the government, the Shabiha. He talked about how the government had created monsters in the various opposition parties as a means of justifying its violence against them.

He wept as he told the story of his imprisonment, torture, and humiliation. He said that the security gangs had arrested most of the men and women of his family, that they had raped three women in front of their eyes and ignored the men's pleas to kill them so they could be spared witnessing such atrocities. Their pleas only fueled the Shabiha's violence, and they were forced to watch their wives, sisters, cousins, and mothers raped.

He said that death would have been more merciful. He noted that the Shabiha later released them after killing two, one who was a defector, and the other the head of his family, who was famous for his generous affection toward homeless children.

How can one convince these men not to take up arms and descend into the cesspool of war that the regime is pushing? How can they be convinced by slogans and chants when the prison spat them up long ago onto the battlefield, to become monsters seeking revenge for their lost dignity and the abuse that befell them and their relatives?

He said, with tears in his eyes, that they weren't asking anyone else to arm themselves and fight. But who could blame them for arming themselves and fighting the occupying forces? Would we be able to remain silent and rational if what had happened to them—to their mothers and sisters, their people, and their city—happened to us and ours?

He concluded his speech by saying that he was unable to go on fighting, so instead he took his weapon and crouched in the rear, looking to aid the wounded. But the scorched earth beneath them was a clear sign that their resistance was failing, so they had withdrawn, aiming to regroup and better prepare themselves for future battles. He said, "We surrender our faith to God's hands and accept His judgment and decision."

I think about the topic of surrender, of helplessness and contentment, and of how a person needs faith to save him from his losses, and to relieve him of the burden of having survived after the departure of his family and loved ones. He needs the miracle of belief so he can enjoy moments of calm and tranquility, the belief that there is someone who will correct the wrongs done to him and return his stolen rights, so that he will ultimately be victorious.

I think the tendency to contemplate murder is a common one, always present in the human psyche, and that it's triggered by circumstances that test a person's patience. These circumstances differ from person to person. Some are more predisposed to violence and murder. They are quick to respond to calls to right wrongs and take revenge for something that was done. They are also constantly looking for enemies, at times even seeing enemies where none exist, as outlets for their aggression and violence. And there are those who are good at setting barriers and deterrents between themselves and the situation at hand, thereby ensuring they have distance to calm themselves and turn away from the choice of violence.

Perhaps thoughts about murder, and attempted murder, are among those neuropsychological issues that are difficult to comprehend. Despite studies of criminal psychology that attempt to better understand murder, reality surprises scientists with new killers who have different psychologies that fool those around them into thinking they're angels who would never hurt a fly, let alone a human being. But the truth surfaces when they transform into killers, when no medical analysis or characterization of instability is useful.

I feel guilty for merely thinking of murder. I constantly remind myself that once, in a traitorous moment, I thought of killing someone. Regardless of how faint that thought was as it flickered in a corner of my soul, in that evil part of me, I cannot move past the fact that I could have been responsible for spilling someone's blood, for wasting their life. And this is not a matter of fear of punishment as much as it is that tingling of conscience that shakes a person and drives them to madness.

This begs the question: How can killers live with themselves?

I have no doubt that it is easy to turn a person into a monster, but is it equally easy to restore that monster to its original human condition? Throughout our miserable, bloody, and violent human history, monsters have been created by murderers and criminals, and unleashing them into society is a step toward destroying the future of civilization and making sin, guilt, and criminality run rampant in societies, so that everyone finds themselves drowning in murder and brutality.

I remember the verbal harassment my wife endured, the drunk's attempt to disrupt our family, and how we discussed this obstacle and overcame it together. Then I mourn our terrible reality, where a simple person can turn into a monster because there is no one else to protect his humanity, lost on the doorstep of historical revolution and daily modern atrocities. And I ask myself: How can I possibly persuade those who have lost everything, lost their families and loved ones, to be patient and believe in divine justice while they see criminals and killers at large in society, carrying flags of blood set on destruction and murder?

The destruction of souls and deformation of lives is one of the most serious threats to our reality, and it the most pressing threat to our future. Healing from these horrific scenes will take a long time. It requires a person to withdraw into himself, lick his wounds, and close his eyes and heart and mind. He must keep himself from remembering those who have departed on a journey in search of the lost, scattered, and wasted humanity.

These Countries

These countries are now far from me geographically, but they continue to inhabit my soul and lead me down corridors of the past and into the maze of memory. They force me to follow the daily news of escalating tragedies as I let out an inward scream that turns into a teardrop that I quickly wipe off my cheek before anyone sees it.

In those countries, you can lose your life for the simplest reason, or for no reason at all. There is no value to human life there, no value to individuals. I recall one of the residents of Amuda saying that the cheapest things in the city was human beings. Everyone and everything was treated as dispensable for the sake of defending that which was more important and supreme. I don't know what that could be, however, for nothing is more important than humans and humanity.

Death awaits you at every corner, alley, and street. Nothing can protect you. A stray bullet could kill you, or an unknown masked man, or some people could kill you in revenge for something you don't know or understand. The chain of possibilities is long, but a natural death is the smallest possibility during a time when death is handed out like chiclets.

Even before the war, people were a cheap commodity in those countries, worthless in the eyes of the regime. Any person who dared to defy the regime would be disposed of publicly, in broad daylight. War only made the daily rate of killings increase, and no one in the civilized countries tried to stop the slowly escalating massacre.

War became the direct cause of death for large numbers of people. Before that, individuals were killed gradually. They would first lose the source of their livelihood, then struggle to make ends meet, then lose their humanity and what it carried of rights and duties. It was essential to keep the sense of defeat ever-present and constantly growing in people who never understood or experienced the true meaning of citizenship in their country.

On more than one occasion, I came close to losing my life. I would get pushed or tricked into such moments in a way that almost made it seem as though they were my predestined fate. Their real causes would be entirely ignored or dismissed with some miserable argument.

A short interview with an Arab newspaper led to my banishment from my city of Amuda to that awful village. It was my punishment for daring to speak out against our experiences of humiliation and dehumanization. I said then that we lived in a country where opportunities were almost nonexistent: opportunities for life and its trappings, of any kind.

The investigator was out to frame me, ridicule me, and devalue the nobility of the art of writing, thought, and literature. His pistol, resting on his desk, was a symbol of his strength and superiority. He repeated that I should be brief and direct in my answers to his questions about my statements in the newspaper, and he stopped me at every word to ask about the intention behind it and my authority on the matter.

He insisted that my words were loaded with hidden meanings, but that he understood the truth of it. That I wanted to display my audacity in criticizing authority, seeking moral favor and imagined heroism, which is something the authorities would not allow me to obtain. The system also would not do me the favor of making me an imaginary hero in the eyes of people who might admire my words and actions, but who would prefer to retreat to a distance from me and from the headaches that might come from dealing with me.

He asked what I thought Arab culture lacked, and I answered that it lacked criticism. I said it needed to recover from paralysis, to stop blaming others for its problems, to separate politics from education, freedom from the whims of cultural conquest. I said it needed a cultural revolution in all senses.

My answer opened the gates of hell. The interrogator began to hurl insults and threats, promising to cut out my tongue and calling me a coward who hid behind the innuendo and metaphors. He said that the state—he meant the system and its security apparatus—had the right to terminate and cut and connect anything, and that all I had to do was submit to its policies, because ultimately it knew best. He stressed that I was a conspirator against the state, an accomplice to the enemy, and that I was weakening the psyche of the people and spreading rumors among them.

He described me as a supporter of normalization with the Zionist enemy. He said I saw Israel as an ally and supporter of my writing and not as an enemy, as I should. He said that when I called for liberation from what I described as the illusions of cultural invasion, I was really calling for the erasure of Arab identity and for opening the channels of normalization with the enemy, who would invade the country and destroy it and everyone in it.

He left no room for me to explain that what I had meant by my earlier statement. I wanted to say I was referring to the need for self-confidence, for history, culture, and the present, and that the power of knowledge should be the leader, supporter, and protector of a nation. It should not be an emptiness that was amplified by hollow, useless slogans.

"Cultural revolution, you son of a dog...?! Who are *you*, dwarf, to call for a revolution?! Damn you and everything about you. Do you think you're a writer, a novelist? The revolution led by our immortal father continues, and we are committed to freeing our country of the enemy's spies and from the intellectual influences of Zionists like you... You want to call for the destruction of the political leadership and its sacred directives? And for a revolution, too?!"

The investigator was raging and steaming as he arranged his curses and insults and exaggerated his promises. He did not beat me; he only intended to hurt me with words, to scare me. I later learned that someone had previously interceded with an officer in the branch and paid him a sum of money so that he would not do me any physical harm, since my body could not tolerate torture and beatings.

In my interview with the newspaper, I had responded to the question, *What are you lacking in your country on the cultural level, seeing as how there are no institutions concerned with the writer except for framing, censoring, and limiting him, and no platforms that operate except with a mob mentality?*

When I remember those miserable and difficult days, I marvel at how I was able to endure all that abuse without any thought to becoming a vengeful killer with powerful connections to the intelligence agencies. I'm not saying that I had risen above revenge, but rather that I found myself preoccupied with other concerns and more important matters, and that my aim was never to take revenge on a victim. I also thought of these investigators as victims of their own circumstances . I lamented their condition and their delusions about themselves and their world.

Suddenly, he looked up at me, smiling. "Finally, you said something right! I agree with you a hundred percent." He was referring to another question the reporter had asked me, "Was there any advice you were given that you didn't take?", which at the time I had answered, "Don't get married."

He was happy with my answer and explained that he was unhappily married, and we were the same in that respect, that there was nothing greater and more enjoyable than single life. He praised the freedom that single men possessed, without a woman to nag them and meddle in their days. He left me no room to tell him what I really thought about the idea behind that piece of advice, and how I believed that every person, in the end, lived their own life and acquired wisdom and experience from it, away from any advice.

Instead, I said, "Freedom is definitely the greatest thing, and it must always be glorified." Aware that my statement might carry a double meaning, he quickly resumed his stern expression and his habit of insulting me and my words, and I went back to lamenting him and his kind. I told him, "You do your work and I'll do mine."

Some people preferred to live in that servitude, imagining that they were in a historic paradise. They were unable to imagine that, instead, they could be the masters of themselves and their own decisions, be independent without having to seek value through following orders. In this case, the self is mired in a complex ordeal. The self is reflected back by the mirror of the ego, as a distorted image, while the ego itself is lost in the thick fog of identity.

Those who are addicted to slavery cannot enjoy freedom. They oppose those who challenge the oppressive regime, describing them as crazy and stupid for fooling themselves into thinking that they might, through their meager efforts, undermine the power of a regime that coordinates with the strongest intelligence services in the world.

The interview that caused my exile, my transfer, my insult and injury, passed through the newspaper like all the other daily conversations that were being published, and no one realized that it had changed the entire course of my life, taking me out of calm and safety and into anxiety, tension, and torture. It also caused my wife chronic anxiety and tachycardia.

Ironically, I ran into the reporter who interviewed me for that newspaper a few years later at the Cairo International Book Fair. I told him how that short interview, which he published in the paper's cultural section, had changed the course of my life and caused me a lot of problems. He smiled and said he didn't remember the interview. I smiled in turn and walked away. "See you later."

I didn't expect him to make up for what had happened to me because of that interview, but his disregard harmed me just as much as the investigator once had. I felt this insult crush my soul, since he who was supposed to value the written word, and to recognize its worth and responsibility, somehow denied it. This brought to mind a Kurdish saying, "Some people talk out of their mouths, and some out of their asses."

It was enough for me to smile at him and turn away. I was turning my back on the reality in which the investigator played the role of interpreter, reading between the lines, reading what was in the heart. A reality in which a poet had no appreciation for the written word, and for its value and worth. Instead, he diluted values, and therefore was more dangerous to art, literature, and thought than the murderers and the ignorant.

The Young Shepherd and the Turkish Military

Our childhood was a flood of warnings. We were never sure where they had come from or why, such that anything might turn against us. We would leave our homes, driven out by those threats, and return to the tune of promises. And so our childhood was snatched from us, with no warning, no planning or awareness, and we were treated as adults even though we had not yet reached puberty.

Never discuss grown-up matters. Be careful not to speak Kurdish at school. Stay away from the police and intelligence officers and never argue with them. These were the daily warnings at the heart of our lives, and we were expected to follow them without really understanding why.

I discovered the contradiction in which my reality drowned, and I in turn drowned in it. And I discovered the division between home and school, for my life at home, on the streets, and everywhere else was in Kurdish, except when I entered school. In school, I had to learn to speak and write in Arabic. We accepted this matter simply and quickly and dealt with this reality as inescapable, unchanging.

In the summer, we were expected to help our families at home. Most of our homes included a number of goats, sheep, or cows, and these animals were the wellsprings of milk and cheese and all other dairy products that were the source of our families' incomes. As the eldest son in a house with three older sisters, I had to carry many of the burdens that I felt took me out of my milieu.

I would walk the goats with other children, who also turned into shepherds after school, and we'd go to the nearby plains and gather our animals and set them free in the pastures. Then we'd break up into two teams. We often lacked a real football, so we would make our own by stuffing some cloth or a big sock with rubber balls or some grass, and we'd have fun playing football barefoot. We would wage our childish battles in the plains that were pastures for our animals, football pitches for us, and lands for our fierce struggles.

There were times when one of us would have to run after his lost animal, which had strayed from the herd to the plains close to the Turkish border, which was a dangerous line of terror that we should never think of approaching. The warning that our parents always repeated was: Never graze near the border, despite the abundance of pasture, because the danger the Turkish border posed was greater than any temptation the pastures might offer.

It was a hot afternoon when the sound of shooting rang out, and a few bullets flew from the rifle of a Turkish military man at the border toward our young friend. It seemed the Turk could not tolerate the shepherd boy following his little herd so close to the barbed wire, or the boy's bravery, so he entertained himself by turning the child into target practice for his sniping and shooting skills.

Not only did the Turkish man kill the boy, but he shot a flare at the straw-covered ground where our friend fell, setting him on fire along with the straw that became his shroud. The charred remains of the assassinated child were later collected from the ashes of the burning bed of straw.

After that incident, our grazing style changed, and our families' treatment of us also changed. We were no longer young shepherds. It seemed, instead, we were potential targets of great enemies such as the soldier who assassinated the child, who would not have hesitated to terminate others if they had approached his guard post.

An atmosphere of bereavement spread through the town. The torched body confirmed that the child had remained far from the border, more than several hundred meters, where he had been frightening some of his quarrelsome goats into returning to him by waving his stick. But it appeared that, nonetheless, the Turkish soldier punished him for daring to allow his flock to approach the wires and for his indifference to risk.

This incident let us know that the matter was graver than our parents' routine warnings and repeated threats, and there were many mysterious things we could not yet understand, and so we had to adhere to the adults' instructions and stop our arguing and complaining. But that state did not last long. We soon grew busy and went back to our old tomfoolery.

I remember details of events that took place before this incident, and how we cheated death many times, or how the Turkish soldiers stationed nearby would overlook our innocent childish quarrels when we—that is, me and my mischievous friends—would raid some bird nests near the barbed wire, or when we would play in the sand of the little valley known as The Valley of the Pig, or its waters or mud. We would take shelter in the long grass, where we'd crawl to our distant targets and lie there under the railway, which we normally saw from afar. We experienced the excitement of having the train pass right above us on the bridge, and we heard the creaking of its wheels and the noise that trailed in its wake. It gave us a tremor mixed with fear: the thrill of adventure, and wonder.

We never told our parents about how close we got to the border, or about our hunting trips and crazy adventures. We conspired with each other to keep our joyful little secret, but after we saw the fire destroy our friend's body, we never broached the topic again. And while the feeling of crossing the line to the other side kept nagging at us, and our curiosity ate away at us, the fear was much stronger. So we ignored these trips and left the birds' eggs alone to hatch in peace. But we never again felt a real sense of safety. We remained captives of our anxiety and fear of the Turkish border and the man who was stationed there, always aiming his rifle at us.

The image of Mustafa Kemal Ataturk was engraved on the hill facing our city, on the Turkish side. On the Syrian side, there an image of Hafiz al-Assad. We children would call it "the hill of Kamaliyah," which our parents would quickly correct with either "It's the hill of Amuda" or "the hill of Darit." History and geography played a major role in our reality. For even though we children did not understand much about concepts and terms, or political and linguistic conflicts, we knew the difference between our words and the words used by the occupying force.

We were positioned between two large suffocating pictures, each linked to an opposing authority who also cut off our air. Each authority outlawed our language, tried to separate us from ourselves and tempt us away from our people. I was not aware at the time of this horror and abuse, but reality shocked us each time with a new truth that made one thing clear: we were treated with hostility and repression by those in power.

We were the hostages and victims of that fence. We often heard strange stories about our people, our uncles and aunts and relatives who remained on the other side, those who spoke and wrote in Turkish. We were eager to meet them and discover their distant-yet-near world, but the horror of approaching the border kept us away. The sight of our friend's burned body remained fresh in our imaginations, and later it turned into a nightmare that kept us from sleep. Sometimes, I would wake up screaming from a dream where I was the burning child in a bed of straw, and that it was my family who had suffered that fatal disaster.

"I readied my horse the day my eyes saw the sun," is a saying that expresses the burden of responsibility one bears at a young age, such that childhood falls hostage to responsibilities, and one finds oneself struggling under their weight. It is a saying that applies to our innocent childhood, full of contradictions and conflicts that we had no hand in—yet still we found ourselves neck deep in its swamps, which later engendered a more painful and bloody reality.

What a brutal childhood we had. What a world we lived in! Why wasn't there anyone who cared to protect our childish innocence?

Many such questions remain stuck in a dimension of time that is disconnected from both the past and the future.

Dialogue of Civilizations

What separates us is much more than what unites us. We must set aside the cunning trickeries that we use on ourselves and others. To what extent does this statement apply to reality? Why should we seem to get along when our grudges are embedded deep beneath our false smiles? Is the myth of brotherhood a lie like any other? Should one seek to root out lies and patch the gaps that reality creates with its continuous shocks?

The mission of literature and art is described as humanitarian, and there are some who hem in the writer, demanding he achieve what these literary police describe as entertaining and beneficial. Books keep you company when you are lonely. But is this the role of literature? What if the author chooses to sprinkle some salt on the wounds in an effort to sound the siren? Why must literature cover up reality's ugliness?

Some writers are accused of exaggerating and inventing drama for the sake of livening their plot, connecting the network of their characters and crafting their destinies. But reality is chock full of coincidences that surpass those in any literary fiction. Others are accused of being too direct, of breaking the rules of dramatic rhetoric, which call for hints and suggestions. What is between the lines is no less important than the lines themselves. What is in our chests needs to be developed into images and embodied into scenes, and then the author must indicate what we should see of the hidden.

The journey of any writer or artist with his followers is the journey of a hunter with his prey. The latter is given just enough to keep their suspense piqued and their attention on the work until the end. The writer casts bait after bait, drawing the reader into his worlds. He draws what he wants, what he promises, what he misses, what provokes him, and all these cause the reader to turn pages in search of hidden secrets.

The literary and art market is mostly steered by a few publishers and businessmen. Work that should be at the top of the publicity list falls behind, and in its place is work that paves the way and removes obstacles for its writer or artist. Coincidence may also play a role in the dissemination of certain works.

In every market, there is someone who designates himself as a gatekeeper. He decides what is and isn't wanted, and what might be wanted, drawing a scheme for people's supposed desires and orientation, which he guesses. In every field, in every time and place, there is darkness, chance, and necessity for those who fill the void and holes, who provide balance. We meet the market's needs—or that is what everyone repeats.

Dialogue of civilizations, dialogue of cultures, and dialogue of religions. This supposed dialogue—intentionally and unnaturally added to civilizations, cultures, and religions—is nothing more than a means of defrauding oneself and others. Everyone knows that the whole issue is naught but a respectable hoax and historical lie that isn't fooling anyone, but they persevere in employing it with a kind of well-practiced sincerity that makes them look innocent.

What dialogue and reconciliation are they talking about, when the conflict is at its peak, getting fiercer and more violent with each passing day? Why has the intensifying war remained hidden since the dawn of history, a war that will continue until civilizations collapse, cultures disappear, and religions disperse? How can we have dialogue when alliances are growing fast, seeking victory?

Perhaps it would be fair to describe these dialogues that are constantly called for as the hypocrisy of cultures, the clash of civilizations, and conflicts of religions. You see them gathering here and there, the patriarchs of delusion, the elders of discord, the religious leaders of blood and madness. Each side considers themselves the most suitable, the best and most virtuous, and when they sit with their opponents under the slogan of brotherhood, they hide the deadly hatred inside them. Hate seems to be the engine of humanity, and people are the fuel of war that has always been. Hatred is everlasting.

Media coverage, allegations, and patchwork. I remember the expression "to cover with a quilt," which we used in my town. Because it was so simple, it was used to describe the so-called dialogue that everyone was ranting about in public, while they stoked the fires of grudges in secret.

Another example from my town came during someone's wedding night. The party was at its peak, and it was time to present the bride and groom with gifts. Khalil's daughter chose that moment to tell her father that her sick little brother had passed away. Khalil did not let himself think long about it before he told her to hurry and cover it with a quilt, that there was nothing wrong with waiting until the gifting ceremony had ended. Khalil's mind cursed the inappropriate timing of death, but he didn't worry over it too much. Rather, he continued to party as though nothing had happened.

It seems that quilt-covering is the hallmark of the dialogue of civilizations and religions, and among the interlocutors who parade by as though they are the representatives of killer gangs lying in wait for each other. Each religious and cultural façade hides a picture of Khalil as he collected his monetary gifts and continued with his party, in order to achieve his financial goal.

Fighting remains the only constant through time and the different types of hatred. The media rushes to advertise ways to patch up facades and hide the opponents' shame, as in reality they continue to quarrel. They exaggerate propagandistic pictures, which are based on fake smiles and pale representations, while behind the scenes there is a sea of indecision, hatred, and anger that blinds everyone and leads to death and murder through hidden incitements and by criminalizing the opposing parties.

Predetermined prejudices are historical shackles and inflamed wounds that ooze pus. Bloody greetings and violent smiles. Any propaganda meeting for any alleged dialogue is essentially a summary of the cover story. Everyone proceeds with the ceremony while they ignore the hatred and put off burying the dead.

This world is nothing but a black market. Glory remains in the grasp of the merchants of souls and arms, and wealth is attained by those who fuel hatred and start wars. The rules of the black market require continuous clashes, while always keeping potential wars on standby for when they are needed.

The dowry of the future is a river of blood and homelands built in cemeteries. What future should we aspire to while we're surrounded by the remains of our lost humanity? Every detail, no matter how small, seems to have its own market. And the declared market, the shadow market, is the one known as black. It's as though a double meaning is necessary for the word to be complete, and the circle closes with openness to that which is desired but forbidden.

Supply and demand govern the course of life in this major market. While millions are preoccupied with the details of their lives and futures, there are those who sit in air-conditioned offices and, using detailed maps, run major laboratories and factories, planning how to spend and export their goods and businesses. They don't care for the people who will fall victims to their tactics—in fact, they gladly offer them as sacrifice. They speed up the immediate collapse in order to protect themselves from the ultimate, inevitable collapse that is successfully postponed by achieving progress. They regenerate, regaining their strength much like vampires who feed on their victims' blood.

The market does not recognize human sentiment. It continues on its trajectory of destruction, toward creating legends. Humans are mice, experiments, numbers, tactics, merchandise, trade, surplus value, a tipping point in the balance of profit and loss. They are what resurfaces and what should be disposed of while reclassifying files and rearranging repositories.

The world is a black market. We must all scream this unchanging fact. We must be as innocent and bold as the child who saw the king naked and shouted about what he saw with his own eyes.

Sometimes, discovering the cure can have a more tragic impact than not having one at all. When the cure remains unknown, the hope of finding it is strong. Yet when it is discovered and people realize the impossibility of obtaining it, their wrath reaches new heights, as the cure belongs only to murderers, who distribute toxins to their victimized masses and prevent them from obtaining medication and treatment.

Bait makes the market possible. When we were young and would hunt birds, we would bait traps to catch them. Our traps were diverse, made in various ways and with varied materials. We used small iron traps to hunt the seasonal and colorful birds. For us, spring was the month of killing birds, the month of polluting innocence and assassinating beauty. It seems that its effects were continuous in more than one sense and flavor.

We would search the barns that each house in our small town had. We'd dig at the edges of humid spots, looking for worms to stimulate the birds' appetites with their wiggling and spiraling movements in the trap.

Worms were the bait we used to tempt birds into our traps. And the birds that we caught were used as bait to attract their families. We used those birds in our games of vengeance, for the kid who hunted the most birds had bragging rights over all others. At times, these games grew heated and led to fights that ultimately led to more hunting trips.

We are the worms used to feed the prey. At best, we are the birds used to attract other birds to the trap, so that they get stuck along with us. We are the worms and the birds. We are the hunters who lost our traps and destroyed the spring.

In Black

Are people's stories secrets that the writer should keep, never to speak of or write about so as not to disclose them or reveal the identities of the people to which they belong? Such stories could be used as means of social pressure on people who confided in the writer, trusting him with parts of their tales. Yet his imagination will seek to fill in the gaps and bridge the distances between events, ideas, and personalities in order to creatively present them. It will work to remain true to the core of the original stories and their tellers, while also branching out to include others. In so doing, the story ceases to be a scandal and becomes a revelation, without exposing anyone or revealing the particular truth of what happened to them or what was in their minds.

Transitioning from being an asylum seeker to being a refugee is a step in the direction of reconciling with the refuge, the self, and the other. It is a threshold on the path to stability that is impossible to achieve during the first years of asylum and may require great time and effort. Hope is cut off for some who seek it. They find themselves exhausted along the way, overcome by pain for their present and frustrated with the progress toward their desired independence and stability.

The asylum seeker finds himself in a large prison, moving within it with what he considers to be freedom. But in reality, he is trapped on all sides. It is a stage that resembles the training young men go through in Syria, during their military service. During that time, they experience hardships and pressures that would make any person despair.

In some cases, the asylum seeker is forced to remain in a specific area where he is placed under permanent supervision. He wears a bracelet that resembles a watch or an electronic anklet that alerts the police to his location.

When a refugee is granted residency, he becomes officially recognized as a person with rights and duties. He finds himself in a wider circle, following a different route, full of endless papers. He must adhere to many appointments he receives from various official departments. He moves up from the five-pound stage to the ten-pound stage.

Five pounds is the daily allowance of the asylum seeker. When he obtains residency, the number doubles, but then he is also required to pay his bills if he chooses to settle in a house, and he is also expected to search for ways to be frugal. The strange thing is, there are people who save up the money they receive for living expenses to spend later in some other way, such as sending some to their families or keeping a portion for later necessities. As for how they manage to survive on whatever is left, well, that is another matter entirely.

I have met people who remained lost, drifting from one church to another and one food bank to another, dropping out of donation places and living off crumbs they gathered from here and there. They convinced themselves that they were doing this for the sake of integration, that they were improving their language skills by mingling with people, but in reality, they were looking for a morsel to satisfy their hunger, that hunger that kept them prisoners of the food banks, free baskets, and organizations.

I knew a person who swore that no penny that entered his pocket would ever leave it, and that he would save it up until, ultimately, he became rich. He lived and breathed money, and his hobby was counting it and smelling the bills. And because he would always eat and drink the same thing, he became so unhealthy that he almost fell ill with stomach diseases. He lost more than twenty-five kilos but pretended that it was intentional, that he had been meaning to lose weight for a long time, and thus his asylum was a heaven-sent gift helping him carry out his diet plan. His health deteriorated so much that he was unable to defecate as a result of his malnutrition and dependence on dry foods. His dry, pale skin was a clear sign of his miserable condition, but he would always smile as he patted the pocket that contained his money, with which he bought a new cellphone that he sent to his wife to assure her that he'd made the right decision to immigrate, and to assure her that he was well on his way to wealth. He did not care that he was losing himself and that he might develop a chronic disease as a result of his passion for money.

Another person I knew could not quit smoking, but his love for money outweighed anything else, so he entered a furious struggle with himself and his fatal love for smoking. He would frequent stores that sold smuggled cigarettes, trying to get them for a lower price, or he would roll his own thin cigarettes and mix dried tea leaves into the tobacco. His cough echoed throughout the house, and his pale skin was a clear sign of his illness, but he was happy with the little money he saved.

Of course, some would buy a one-pound lottery ticket twice a month, hoping they would hit the jackpot and become millionaires. Illusions guide many asylum seekers who waste money despite the restrictions imposed on them, squandering part of the money that wasn't enough in the first place, but which was meant to keep a person just at the threshold of hunger and deficiency and a hostage to despair, frustration, depression, and self-contempt.

These compensations and food stamps are meant to provide temporary relief to refugees for whom food is in short supply and who cannot manage their shelter and livelihood. However, they have become an addiction for many refugees, who are haunted by the accumulation of crumbs they believe will make them rich in the future.

There are also refugees who think they are simply here in a transitional phase, between leaving their homeland and returning. You see them saving some of the money that would have kept them just above the poverty line and sending it to their country. The amount given to them is carefully calculated by the government, which considers it enough to meet the refugee's needs without allowing him room for entertainment.

These people prefer to collect the money and send it to their countries to buy real estate or gold, to enjoy the feeling of illusory wealth while living in the shell of poverty, fear, need, and inferiority. They convince themselves that, as strangers and refugees, they are supposed to consider their future and the future of their children and to strive to achieve something, or at least to overcome the hardships of the near future. Yet what they don't admit to themselves is that they use the money to pursue passion and enjoyment and do not pay attention to their own endless losses.

As for the government program intended to resettle Syrian refugees, the matter is different. The applicants to this program did not go through the same steps as the asylum seekers and refugees entering the country, whether legally or illegally. So there are some who believe themselves to be in a strong, central position. They boast that, among the refugees of yesterday and today, they are "more worthy" of the aid and opportunities than those brought in through the United Nations' refugee settlement program.

There are those who seek to improve their lives and think about their futures here in a way that agrees with the country's social system. They don't want to remain on the sidelines, so they try their best to improve themselves and their language skills and to search for work. Meanwhile others look at their host country in a different way, as though the aid provided to them is meant to stay safe and secure and never to leave their pockets under any circumstances. They make plans to use the money for their second start in their home country and to better their lives back there. By then, they imagine, they'll have accumulated enough wealth to guarantee them respect and appreciation from those around them.

Fear of poverty, fear of hunger, and fear of fear itself prevents the refugee from coming to terms with himself. It keeps him bound to his illusions of wealth, money, and appreciation. It keeps him living in the shadow of food stamps and alms offered by this or that organization. Some also believe that by frequenting humanitarian organizations and becoming acquainted with the people who work there—those who help the poor and refugees—they're making a good connection. But they don't think of making these connections for the sake of human or social interaction, but rather as a way to get more money.

Sometimes donations are collected to send to Syrian refugees in the camps, but there are also refugees who collect these donations with the excuse that they're in need. They take more than they need from these donations so they will appear generous to others and call attention to themselves as generous givers. But they never think of how they are taking money away from people who really need it, people who are hungry and cold, living in refugee camps elsewhere.

The tricks some refugees resort to because they fancy themselves smarter than everyone else don't really fool anyone. They look at their lives in the country of asylum, in addition to being temporary, as a way of searching for wealth, but not for meaning. "Black market job" is a phrase that commonly passes among them. That is, to work outside the country's legal framework, unregistered in the work center, without a signed contract or any other niceties. Black market jobs are one of the ways they are convinced they can get rich in Europe, because, in this way, a person can keep his entire salary while still collecting unemployment checks and aid from the government. They imagine themselves sipping from a spring dripping with money, while they overlook the time creeping out of their hands and holding them hostage to the black market, to a black future.

There are those who work in the black market and keep their money at home. They avoid depositing it in the bank out of fear that they'll be asked where they got it. They are afraid of investing their money, because they don't want to be questioned about their sudden wealth, which might draw attention and suspicion. They prefer to accumulate money and wait for the right time to spend or invest it, but, through all this, they are afraid of their own shadows, of their imaginations, and of the money itself. Their anxiety can turn into an obsession. They constantly worry that someone might find out about the money they're hiding, or that they might be robbed, perhaps even by the people closest to them. They would never dare report the theft to the police or complain about it, because then they'd put themselves under suspicion, making themselves accountable for that money. They would have to explain why they hadn't disclosed it to the government in the first place. Black market money could disappear in one black night and become a nightmare for its owner, who remains imprisoned by the darkness of his ideas and the weight of constant suspicion in himself and in those around him. The temptation of black-market money is often the worst trap.

One former refugee who had been living in Britain for almost three decades spoke to me about the successes and achievements he'd had in his studies and work, and about the situations he'd come across through his work aiding new Kurdish and Arab refugees in the UK. He expressed his shock at the large number who came with miserable ideas about the social and economic lives of the people of the country and its refugees.

After helping the newly resident refugees establish a stable life—without asking for them to compensate him for his money, time, and effort in helping them set up their new homes—he would have one shock after another. It quickly became clear that the refugee had the impression that his life would run easily and smoothly from this point on, that he would not need to exert any effort to better himself or to find a job. Some would describe government aid as a fixed salary and imagine the wealth they would accumulate in a short period of time, before turning around and going back to their country to make a stable, luxurious life for themselves that would earn him other people's appreciation and accolades.

He was disappointed, he said, to discover the simplicity and superficiality of his countrymen's thinking. He would hear them express disappointment with their host country, saying they had expected a paradise but that, alas, it had not met their expectations. They complained that the aid was not enough for them to buy land and real estate in their home country, as they'd hoped, or to take a second, younger, and more beautiful wife.

One day, the veteran refugee made up his mind to buy a gift for a countryman. He visited him in the evening with a small broom in hand. He told him, in all seriousness and sobriety, that he had brought it because the next day, the government would throw money on the ground in the public park for refugees to collect. He explained that it was an annual tradition that the government kept up to help new refugees who did not have enough money from the aid they were given to improve their lives, but that it was also okay for non-refugees to join in if they wanted.

This new refugee believed his fellow countryman, even though it felt alien to him. He chalked the strangeness up to cultural difference, which formed a gap that could not be bridged or crossed. He added this to his accumulated life experiences, observations, encounters, traumas, and disappointments. He went to the public park early in the morning, broom in hand and more than one bag in his pocket, hoping to sweep and collect cash from the ground.

The veteran refugee watched as the new refugee waited for the supposed splash of cash, stroking his broom as if he were stroking a horse that would lead him to victory in a historic battle. Then, minutes later, he popped out in front of the new refugee and greeted him sarcastically, "Hey, partner! Have you swept the money up off the ground?" Only then did the new refugee feel the slap inflicted on him by his greed, meant to teach him a lesson and open his eyes to life's realities: that money is not thrown in the streets and that you need to work to make it, not collect it in the black market, but in the colors that give life meaning and grant a person hope.

One of the refugees, a Kurd from Syria, had been in Britain for more than seven years. All this time, he'd worked hard, making money and saving it up, not visiting anyone or allowing anyone to visit him, content with his relationships at work, since he worked about thirteen hours a day at a restaurant. He ate and drank at work, and his house was just a place for him to sleep. His bills were few, and he paid little else in terms of taxes and such. He lived as happily as he could as he saved his money, dreaming of future wealth, of going back to his country and choosing a young wife to acquire with his money. He dreamt of enjoying his life there and, of course, of directing some metaphorical slaps to the people against whom he carried an eternal grudge, a grudge that continued to fester and grow inside him, awaiting retribution and justice.

This was a person whose dreams became nightmares that prevented him from living as an equal human being, keeping him captive to wealth, panting as he sought to collect thousands of pounds so he could live comfortably in the future and enjoy his wealth. He was robbed in broad daylight. One of his co-workers stole his house key straight out of his pocket, at the restaurant where they worked, and went there after work and stole the money he had stuffed in his pillowcase, as old grandmothers used to do. He searched through his cabinets, too, and even took the change this man kept on his kitchen counter. He managed to do all that and return the key to the refugee's pocket without the man sensing a thing.

This lover of money fell into the trap of suspecting everyone around him, and slowly he began to talk to himself, telling the people around him his stories, dreams, grudges, future projects, and long-ago plans. From one story to the next, he would curse, and soon his suspicions turned into an oppressive yoke, and he became a patient afflicted with an incurable phobia, crazy with suspicion. He became famous among the refugees as the bankrupt millionaire, and then as the morbid obsessive. He was used as an example for those who might postpone living life, awaiting a future that could hold bad luck for them as they wasted opportunities in search of an illusion. The last I heard was that he had completely lost his mind. I did not look into the matter further. He remained a figure in the swamp of blackness, constantly imagining his future paradise.

Cairo, the City of Elegance

It is a must, as I write my British diaries, that I return to certain encounters and stops along my path to asylum, exile, displacement, stability… There were some places I passed through that left indelible traces on my soul and my conscience.

I sit in a corner of the library. I watch the cameras planted in the ceiling and the walls, the ones that continuously capture my movements, gestures, and motions. The library appears to be another front for the black market.

Every reader turns into a voyeur, spying on the writer's private life, interpreting every detail. They are like the writer, who is a voyeur himself into life's minute, private details, dissecting and overanalyzing them with a kind of skilled craft and re-creation. The reader turns into a detective of mysteries and secrets of which he knows nothing, but guesses at, as a researcher at an archaeological dig searches for anything he can find. He thinks that anything he finds, an artifact or masterpiece, is a worthy project. Some readers look for a crime committed by the writer; it does not matter who the crime is committed against. What matters is tracing and uncovering the clues.

Interpretation is a built-in error for many readers and writers. It is simultaneously a gateway to the text and a crossing beyond it, such that one appears to be a niche in the dark interior of the other.

This is life: a reservoir of stories and a volcano of novels. One suffers from the excessive flow of strange stories and finds that he cannot adapt to reality at all by referring to imagination and madness. He realizes that he must face the facts by diagnosing them and revealing the hidden in order to deduce a path for treatment and remedy.

A person reaches the point where he feels captivated by the fiery circles pressing on him, restricting his movements and disrupting his imagination. Every detail is sure to be absurd—as though imbalance were a characteristic of all previous and later eras. It's a world of superstition that lives inside humans and leads them to a hell, everyone racing to be the first. A theater of lies and curses, a reality of heartbreaking comedy. A person bargains for what he does not have in an effort to obtain what he will not have. A miserable, vain endeavor. Imagination bleeds sorrow and alienation, a permanent wound in the soul.

Entertainment is one of the goals of literature. Logos and marketing. Each writer markets himself as savior, liberator, and redeemer. Yet the time for entertainment has passed, and now is a time for pain, for peeling away delusions, a time for confrontation and erosion, a time for renewed anxiety and pouring salt on wounds.

"Cairo is the city of anti-elegance," I whisper to my friend, and we give regretful laughs. We are obliged to humor others and be courteous in all situations, for our accents will always expose us. Then people would ask us about the situation in our home country, tell us that they hope for peace in it, and end the conversation by assuring us that we are "the best kind of people."

I write to my friends about Cairo: about its noise, its crisis, the dust that distorts one's vision, and about its extreme anger, among other things. And I never forget to include in my letter that "Cairo is the mother of the world." I write as I laugh: Cairo is Cairo.

I remember parts of the novel *Invisible Cities* by Italo Calvino, in which he describes the characters of dozens of cities in a way that moves the reader among their ruins. Its imagined maps color these cities with many emotions, shapes, and desires, which the reader can choose to recall or forget. I imagine the emperor Kublai Khan looking out over his empire, watching it grow and expand, releasing his envoys and tax collectors to explore remote areas. They return to him, to the gardens of Mongolia, with detailed reports of their trips. He sees the reflection of his empire in a desert that is as variable and unstable as its grains of sand, and he sees in every city and region the shapes previously depicted by Marco Polo, who hailed from Venice and learned the Tartar language soon after his arrival, when he became a companion of the Khan. He satisfied his curiosity for knowledge and discovery by telling him stories of cities and their people. They often debated the value of travel and whether it was necessary in order to discover the other. Khan asked, "Are travels a way to relive the past?" This is a question that could be rephrased as, "Is travel a way to obscure the future?" Marco answered that, in other places, one found a dark mirror that enabled him to see little of what he had and much of what he did not, and would not, possess.

Imagination took them far. Polo swore to him that every person carried in his mind a city made up of differences, a city without numbers or form, filled with special towns. There are two types of cities: those that remain constant over the years and give form to desires, and those temporary cities that either wipe out desires or that are erased by human desire. He spoke to him of fortified cities that could not be subjugated, of hidden cities that were made up of forms, voices, and movements that you could feel but not see. These cities brought to mind visions of departed souls, suggesting past situations and events that the reader could invoke and imagine.

Marco told the Khan not to confuse cities with the words used to describe them, because there were many connections between cities, and falsehood appeared in objects, not in words. A city might summarize all other cities, while some cities appeared gray, lacking in character and color, created with no purpose. The cities imagined in the dreams of Kublai Khan appeared as kites, pointed like spears: mobile, striped, ornate, weaving relationships like a cobweb that almost resembled an identifiable shape or incarnation. He looked for details and particles to complete the image in his mind, while at the same time fearing he might lose the other cities he spoke of or imagined.

What description applies to this city that conceals from us more than it shows? Are we about to discover it? Is it possible to penetrate its details and get to know it more closely? Why is this so difficult for us when the city itself appears to be simple and clear? Will it become apparent in some form, some situation? Millions of people live in it, which means that millions of towns make up the city and give access to it. How is it possible to get to know these millions of towns? Each person has his own Cairo, his own city that has either defeated him with passion, or with poverty and starvation. The most important visible bond is this: that the city that is hard to tame is the city that belongs to him.

We suffer from loneliness in our Cairo—we now have all the pieces of it. We miss and lack Cairo as we would a woman, and we feel utterly defeated without her. We miss the presence of a woman by our side, to whom we could speak and who would speak to us, who would remain in our arms at night, keep our bed warm and quell our bodies' hunger.

Haram Street, or Pyramid Street, reflects the blatant dissonance of Greater Cairo. It is parallel to another street to the west, separated by a human island. Some of the people who live there claim that it's located in the neighborhood of the pyramids. They brag about where they live, since the pyramids' neighborhood is considered more upscale than the slums surrounding it. Others like to say that they're on the border between immorality and purity, a reference to the cabarets and night clubs lined up on Haram and Faisal Streets. This description, in turn, identifies the area and reflects its characteristics. And that is what the person describing it is keen to remind the listener of, more than of its spatial aspect. That is, he does not mind enjoying his life to the fullest, as well as acknowledging God's rights over him. He does his homework, plays at the sidelines, and reminds everyone that God is forgiving and merciful.

I remember people's obsession with their pharaohs and pharaonic history. Haram Street reflects that obsession in the form of a present that evokes the names of all those pharaohs who ruled the country in succession. Here, the names of the pharaohs are used for hotels, shops, streets, and cafes. They are even used for tuk-tuks.

And, speaking of tuk-tuks, these are a means of transportation common in Cairo, symbolizing the opposite of Cairo's great metro, which we used to tell ourselves was the most important Egyptian achievement, more important than the pyramids themselves. The tuk-tuk, a three-wheeled motorcycle of sorts, is light and easy to maneuver, yet annoying. It moves through most Cairo streets, swaying in such a way that its rider looks as though he is about to fall off it at any moment. It transports simple things through the city and is not used for long distances. And although it cannot really replace a car or public transportation, it is used to carry out many tasks. They are a nightmare for taxi drivers, who see them as a threat their work and livelihood, but some of these drivers console themselves, as they were previously tuk-tuk drivers who got promoted into cab drivers after they saved up enough money to buy a car, from all their work behind the wheel of a tuk-tuk.

We giggled as we read an ad on a billboard that said: "Nefertiti Smells." We debated the various dimensions of the word "smell" and laughed as we imagined the stench that clogged our noses, the smells that come out the backside and mouth after a person falls asleep, imagining a procession of bad smells sweeping through us and drowning us. The suggestion completely contradicts the magic of the word "perfume," but suggests that the scents intertwine with each other in a way that does not preserve the aesthetic or discretion of any of them.

Aton is not a Pharaoh and is not ruled by anyone; he has no grave to his name and no pyramids or tomb beside the tomb of Sphinx. Aton is an upscale nightclub at the beginning of Haram Street on the Pyramids side. The term "upscale" has a different meaning in Egypt than it does anywhere else. Aton is divided into three floors, each of which has a different entrance, for privacy reasons. To a newcomer, it might seem that there is one Aton, but after entering the establishment, it becomes clear that there are, in fact, three Atons, each with a different entrance fee and gate.

Kissing up, flattery and hypocrisy are some of the characteristics of many who you encounter here. They will exaggerate your importance in the hopes of emptying your pockets. You won't run into anyone who respects himself, deals with you on the basis of mutual respect, and is satisfied with being fair without any underlying greed or intent to rob you.

Many of those who return to visit this country after immigrating say that their brokers swindled and cheated them. They seek out any means to convince and deceive you, using false pretenses and glorified labels, such as "your honor," "your lord," "sir," "captain," "prince," and other titles that give a false aura that dissipates as soon as the broker gets what he wants. And if anyone argues about these things, they will simply repeat "not possible," which they use as a precursor and an ending to every sentence. They employ it so simply and cleverly that it reveals the unalterably practical side of Egyptian collective memory.

I tell myself, as I try to swallow my laughter, that if those pharaohs knew that their names were going to be used in such ways, they would have either committed suicide or stepped down from their positions of power and executed any historian who might have documented their names.

The legacy of the pharaohs is celebrated in a contemporary way; there is a mix of verbal boasting of their Islamic affiliation, with some practices that support this affectation. There is a trade that promotes pharaonic history. It comes to the fore, in conjunction with the pride people take in inheriting the great pharaonic civilization, receiving the keys to the pyramids and the mandate to protect and preserve it. And this preservation comes by neglecting it, as it appears, under the pretext of preserving its brilliance and elegance. But this corresponds to the orientation of some of those who exaggerate their monotheism and Islam. They convince themselves that the pharaohs were the first monotheists ever to believe in one God, but then contradict themselves by describing the pyramids as merely sanctified graves that should be demolished so that the country's historical features become compatible with its contemporary identity, so that any legacy that conflicts with the Sharia should be eliminated.

There is another way to destroy the pyramids and remove them from history, and that is by erasing any aesthetic interest from them and from anything around them, keeping them hostage as a miserable popular tourist attraction where beauty seekers continue to be attracted and workers continue to extort them by selling them overpriced camel rides. These workers speak a few words from several languages, enough to tell the tourist the amount of money they want. They employ courtesy and hypocrisy at the beginning of the exchange, then revert to rudeness and intrusion at the end, after they have taken the tourist's money. Any currency is common and acceptable there, as if the pyramids' yards have turned into a free market open to small tourist guides who derive their strength from influential and powerful people.

Many of those who have visited the pyramids express their disappointment, shock, and remorse for having visited the site, wishing they had kept this bright image in their minds and imaginations, and saying that the pictures they took, which might motivate others to visit, should serve be a condemnation of their dissipated dream, a reminder lest they think of returning to the pyramids again.

I console my Egyptian friend, who bleeds heartache and grief over the conditions of his history and country every time he remembers the scenes of destruction and neglect surrounding the pyramids, and how their surroundings have turned into markets of extreme misery and destruction. I tell him that the value of these monuments must and will be realized later.

I console him as I hush my fear that these monuments may be wiped out and disappear. I console myself and imagine the pharaohs standing on the tops of their pyramids, mourning their history, when they should be watching their past glories advance their country. I imagine the pharaohs seeing the reflection of their achievements in a desert of a variable and unstable nature, like grains of sand, just like the Emperor Kublai Khan. The pharaohs see every buggy, camel rider, horse, and camel as a symbol, a story, and a tragedy without beginning or end.

The sense of beauty is absent here, and only a sense of profit is present. History is collapsing in its ugliest manifestations. Reality is displaying its ugliest manifestations and reality presents its harshest tools. Modernity sweeps through ruthlessly. The Sphinx lies miserably, crying out to his engineers and weeping for the slaves whose blood was spilled to build him.

Perhaps it is the illusion of history and its cruelty, which must show the ugliness of the tourist's delusion upon dreamily entering the pyramids. His dream gives way to illusion and actually harms the innocence of the tourist's dream and strips history of any sanctity.

I repeat to myself, again and again, that it seems Cairo is a city not only hostile to elegance but also hostile to glory and history. Cairo, to me, is the embodiment of a monster eating itself, represented in a volcano ready to erupt and demolish everything around it. She is a hungry mother eating her own children and disposing of their bones in a quick-burning oven that is difficult to escape.

Khufu the Syrian

Khufu, the Syrian.

My name, as saved on an Egyptian taxi driver's cellphone, is: Khufu the Syrian. He asked me to save my name on his phone, just like that, so he would remember who I was when I called him. When he told me this, he was thinking he had just discovered a wealthy new client who would earn him a lot of money for driving him around every day. He stressed that I should remind him of my name when I called so he wouldn't get confused, since his memory was strong but he couldn't read. He went on to explain the reasons behind his illiteracy, blaming everything and everyone. He held the government responsible, the school, his family, the sheikh of his village and the mayor as well, but he forgot to bear any responsibility himself. I didn't want to get into a useless debate with him, especially since my time with him was going to be short. I also didn't want to talk a lot, because speaking over the noise would have required me to yell, and I learned early on that when I raise my voice for more than a few minutes, I get a blinding headache.

I don't quite understand the link between my yelling and headaches, but experience has taught me to avoid going through that again. However, I often find myself breaking the promises I make to myself. It reminds me of the friend who said he has always made plans for himself, from the first grade to college, but has never stuck to any of them. And the thing is, he actually enjoyed breaking them.

I gave in to the funny driver's request and saved my name in his phone just as he requested. He double-checked it by calling me, and he was reassured when my phone rang, thinking he had hooked me as a new customer.

The driver wasted no time and turned right to gossip. He talked about everything he had seen on the road, criticized state policies, analyzed foreign policy, talked about what should be done to revive the country and lift people out of poverty, hunger, begging, and need. He turned to me between topics to make sure I was listening and to check the impact of his comments. I reassured him with a slight nod before looking straight ahead to remind him to keep his eyes on the road. He would smile and tell me that he had all the roads in Egypt memorized.

I envied his Egyptian accent, then I quickly laughed at my envy and rationalized it by telling myself that it stemmed from my exile. I recognized the irony of envying him. I remembered a friend who was always surprised when he encountered foreigners. He would listen to them intently and was in complete awe whenever he saw children speaking a foreign language. He would happily listen to them with passion and eagerness, and he would express his admiration by yelling, "Goodness! These children speak foreign languages so well, and we don't know any ourselves!" He didn't want to listen to any explanation we gave him, such as that the language they were speaking was their mother tongue, just as we had our own mother tongue. He was never willing to discuss it, never convinced by the explanations we gave him.

The driver distracted me from my thoughts when he asked what I thought of what he'd just said, to which I replied, "I agree."

He was pleased with my agreement, even though he'd noticed that I was not really listening to what he was saying, and he went back to his running commentary. He spoke of the wealth that could be gained by exploiting the potential of his country and how it would return to its glory days, as he wanted to recover that greatness and past glory, bringing his country back to the days when it had ruled the world. He wanted the country to create new miracles just as it once had.

He was not a greedy man, unlike his appearance and conversation seems to suggest. For, when I looked at the meter that displayed a price of fifteen and a half pounds, I gave him a twenty, and he gave me five pounds back. I was surprised by his behavior, because I was used to cab drivers asking for more money, not handing extra back. When I told him that I did not have half a pound to give him, he said: "May God forgive you for it, Pasha."

I didn't bother blaming myself for my feelings. The traffic jam at the top of the road made me forget everything. The tuk-tuk brought me back to reality with its sad appearance and movements. I was forced to compare the two most common methods of transportation in Egypt.

As I entered the first gate of the Ahram Gardens, which is called the Khufu Gate, I remembered the driver asking me to save my name as Khufu the Syrian. For a second, I liked that name. I imagined myself as a pharaoh, in a street or neighborhood of a city named after me. Fantasies floated away with me.

Then the new nickname brought me to a subject that had remained a source of stress for me. Every step I took dragged me back to reality.

Identity and its historical consequences on people's thinking: How are identities formed, what are their constituent parts, and where do they lead us? I recalled Amin Maalouf's book *Deadly Identities* and his realistic historical analysis, taken from his personal experience as well as his family's history in a country where many identities continue fighting amongst themselves, sometimes merely for the sake of keeping the conflict alive.

My new nickname brought me back to the questions I used to ask myself, and which I sometimes intentionally would not answer, lest my answers be relative and unconvincing, no matter how persuasive they might be. Perhaps persuasions require masks of their own.

Distorted identities. Fragmented. Lovable. Crazy. Wretched. Lost. Displaced. Murderous. Unidentifiable identities.

My new nickname might be expressive of who I am, and it might be the furthest thing from who I am. Nicknames often stick to us more than our names do. I am not in favor of choosing nicknames, but many of the monikers that we're given gain legitimacy by becoming popular, used by so many that we realize one day that others call us by this or that nickname, and we are unable to ignore or reject it. We either accept it with a smile on our face, or resist it, which only serves to make it more popular.

This echoes my desire to learn about the problematic aspects of identity, while always putting off the exploration. I convince myself to collect as many references as possible, read as much research as possible, and discover what I can in terms of insights, analysis, and theories in order to give the topic its due. After all, many contemporaries and former theorists seem to be occupied with it, and many people seem to regard it as important, the elite and the general public alike, and each addresses the topic from their own angle.

In your country, you are seen as a foreigner, having come from another country less than half a century ago. There, you are also seen as someone ripped away from his roots, since you were born and raised in another country, imbued with its culture and customs. And you, yourself, live both contradictions and belongings.

Geographical terminologies and administrative divisions can restrict identities, label them and make them real. But perhaps they are mere words, contexts that legalize our identity, or restrict and ban it, and fan the flames of the disagreements around it.

I asked myself all this while wondering what I could have been, my supposed identity, under different historical conditions. I wonder whether, if I had a homeland I could point to on a map, I would have remained devoid of identity.

I have my ID card, but this is not my identity. Identity is a thing that lives inside us, travels with us, grows in importance in our minds and hearts, and which we resort to if we are ever threatened with erasure, for it becomes a way for us to prove our roots.

Why do we insist on clinging to our roots? Why do we resort to such depths to fight the horizons? Why do we avoid confronting dangers and threats by entrenching ourselves behind illusions? Is identity only an illusion, or are we mere shadows and ghosts without it?

Questions keep coming to me, triggered by that driver's simple and spontaneous act of nicknaming me Khufu the Syrian. But—am I really a Syrian in the full sense of the word? In Syria, I was always called a Kurd, and that's how I was seen. The bitter irony is that this accusation was made not only by people with power and authority, but also others in everyday life, making tribal divisions.

Khufu the Syrian triggered a history of sorrow within me.

In Egypt, people say "pulling a Kurd on me" when they accuse someone of trying to trick them or take them for fools. The meaning changes if you replace Kurd with Arab or Easterner, for then it refers to closeness, courtship, or involvement in the other's affairs and troubles.

I find that most people use the term without being aware of the racial aspect, which belittles Kurds. When you ask them to clarify the term, they fall into the same trap, referring to Kurds in terms of naivety and ignorance. But this serves to clarify the historical ambiguity that permeates their dialect. They do praise the historical role of the Kurds in Islamic history and talk about the greatness of Saladin in his liberation of Jerusalem. But their clarification of the term remains unconvincing and does little to dispel the pervasive linguistic prejudices.

Before the current map was drawn for the region, the old one looked different. Sykes and Picot divided the area according to their countries' interests. International interests dictated and restricted the borders of several countries, and these maps have become a point of debate for the people who live there. On the one hand, there are those who curse these lines that bind them, while on the other there are people who would protect these lines with their lives. Sometimes they describe them as delusional, a creation of colonialism, while at other times they describe them as sacred and necessary.

After drawing the new map, we missed our old one, to which we'd tied our dreams and nightmares. It haunted us, and yet it restricted us when we followed its rules. A Kurd now carries his map in his heart and mind, and he refers to it in his discussions and presents it as his way of rooting himself in his land, history, and civilization. But that makes others look at him with skepticism and suspicion. They accuse him of inciting independence, or other such accusations that have always kept the Kurdish man a prisoner of his dreams, which may lead him to actual long-term imprisonment.

When you declare your Kurdishness, you are looked on as a separatist, and the burden lies with you to prove the opposite. And if you exaggerate your defense, you will be suspected of hiding your true intentions. The other's confusion is reflected onto you, and you are looked at with doubt.

In our small town, we were bound by our village identity. In the neighboring towns and cities, we were bound by our town's identity. In the big cities, we were bound by the identity of our province. And when pressed for detail, we were bound by our accused yet innocent identity. And when one emigrates and adopts another nationality, his nationality remains incomplete because of his previous identity, which is also in question. One finds himself in a sea of successive identities, set in labyrinthine circles, where identity draws its mazes and circles: from a village identity to a city to a regional to a continental to a religious... And the circles open to each other in a kind of overlap, so that the lines become blurred but controlling.

Is identity a place, a language, a race, a color, a shape, a dream, a desire, a past, a wager, a future?

Is identity the enemy of integration? Is it the mercury to integration's gold? Is it a slowly exploding time bomb? A historic complex that gets continually renewed with its magical effects on division and dispersion?

Identities migrate with us and change with the changes in place and time, but they remain shackles and markers throughout all times and places. It is also a complex problem piled onto many other problems. It may be a constraint, a chasm, or a volcanic eruption. Identity has become a timed minefield in a changing world. I discovered that identities overwhelm people and keep them scattered and confused, and that no one is free from the impact of identity and its alienation.

Conspiracies control our destinies, and thinking about them can make people antagonize all those around them. We did not have the option of being raised this way or that, but some of us tried to break off our leashes and search for answers to questions and to the accusations of others.

I noticed that the identity-centered debates are aimed at restricting rather than erasing boundaries, looking to support the confinement theory, even while it claims to seek to navigate the theory's minefields and barriers.

I comfort myself by thinking about identity as something we live and desire. What we desire to be. However, this does not keep the accusations from growing and multiplying. Accusations come from those who say an identity is not acquired, from those who are accused of estrangement from an identity, and from the ones who question such definitions. The image is more confusing and disturbing than it is comforting.

Everything makes up an identity: form, desire, dreams. That is, we are the product of multiple identities, and it's impossible to limit a person to one specific identity. If you are a Muslim, you are included in a category of religious identity, and if you are also a Kurd or an Arab, then this falls under the category of ethnic identity, and if you are Syrian or Turkish, this falls under the category of national identity. Thus, you find yourself faced with an endless line of identities.

The terrifying obsession with the purity of identity is like a lover's illusion about the purity of his beloved.

Simple facts increase our sadness. I realize that assets do not exist except in the mind, but I also realize that minds are what guide reality and draw its maps, so I am in a sea of murderous identity that is blasphemous, risky, and heretical.

I will remain in Egypt, in the taxi driver's phone, as Khufu the Syrian. I, in turn, saved his name as Khufu the Driver. My new nickname comforted me. Through it, I acquired a new identity that enriches my earlier and later identities. I thanked Khufu for giving me his name centuries after his departure. I go back, searching for him, to discover his greatness.

My friend joking called him the Syrian Sphinx, insinuating effeminacy with the title of Sphinx. I became serious as I defended the matrilineal age and the authority and power of the female, justifying that she had reached such heights of greatness that she immortalized herself and her name in a great pyramid. But I did not want to delve into the authority that chooses a male name for a female so as not to diminish her status and stature. For would masculinity in consciousness appear more influential?

I needed a female Sphynx to share my horror and dispel my estrangement and loneliness, and to warm my cold bed with the originality and civilization of her body.

In a moment of silence, I flipped through the newspaper.

"Looking to hire a live-in maid. Preference given to a Syrian national who works hard."

I broke down in tears as soon as I read this advertisement. Now, my Syrian identity came to the forefront of my psyche and confused me. The driver marveled at my heavy tears, noticing that I was crying when I reached for a tissue from the box in front of him. Although he was surprised by it, he spared me having to answer his questions.

Some wanted her for a maid, others wanted to marry her under the pretext of protecting her and her honor. Everyone held others responsible for the downfall they brought to us. What is disgusting is that there are those who equate action with reaction and call for accountability for reactions before even holding the perpetrator accountable.

I am Khufu the Syrian.

I, the Syrian, am material for advertising, information, begging, and pity. This is what brought us to the false slogans that continue to be traded half a century after the destruction of our homeland. The only slogan people have actually committed to is the burning down of the country and the fragmentation and displacement of its people. The real fall began when people were bombed, and the inevitable subsequent fall was a toll, the payment in blood, its cost as expensive as a homeland.

Each country claims to be the one that gave aid to the refugees first, here or there, and each country claims to be the one that took them in out of a sense of duty, brotherhood, hospitality, and humanity.

Khufu the Syrian.

"Those who have lived in Damascus will never be satisfied living anywhere else," he repeated, heartbroken.

Cultured Feathers

The educated live at Café Riche. Live, live, live. Know-it-alls, charlatans, and windbags... The naïve, the enemy of crowds ... How many sweet words and how much jargon makes up solutions to people's problems....

Oh, Sheikh Imam and Ahmed Fouad Najm, may God have mercy on your souls! In this little song, you have expressed the state of the defeathered intellectual so well.

This song stays with me days after every dutiful visit I make to the café located behind Riche. Café Riche is sometimes referred to as an elite spot, while others would describe it as low-class. That's because it has reasonable prices for visitors and an intimate and familiar atmosphere; that is, the visitor should expect a simple and unchanging atmosphere resembling that of Cairo, which is covered in trash and flies, with beggars moving between tables stealthily and gracefully, practicing their usual ritual.

Their miserable appearance as they hover around the low tables smoking shisha and wearing the revolution's flag around their necks upsets me. When I compare them to women and children who beg, I find them terrible in their blood-trade and their superficial care for their country. They are begging in the name of the revolution, while others are forced to beg because of need. Each of them manages his affairs in their own way. The aid and support they receive constitutes the most important part of the relief efforts. The issue of dissent provides many of them with safe havens away from what they had been suffering, overwhelmed in their fields, or sidelined and unable to attain fortune or get their rights.

When I sit, watching them, I can't help but curse the revolution: If these people are revolutionaries, then the revolution is a whore and a child born of adultery. Then I calm down and tell myself not to lose hope in the faces that swarm my mind, nor in the heroism that I witnessed from simple people who have kept the revolution strong, honorable, and true to a future befitting both revolution and country, which is on the verge of extinction. I do not remember who said that a true hero is often a hero by chance, for he dreams of being an honorable coward like the rest. However, I realize that heroism does not apply to any of the people I see here.

With bitterness and heartache, I recall the words of the song and hum along with it as I quickly wipe away my tears and claim to have dust in my eyes.

A woman puts a handful of unpeeled pistachios on each table, then turns around and revisits each table to collect whatever money the people can spare her. By this method that she invented, she is able to get rid of the usual burden of begging and instead receives comfort and security. She has also formed a protective shield for herself, for she appears to be a street vendor, but her way of selling is different. Anyway, that handful of pistachios is a delicious change, especially when the evening is long and the seated person needs something different to eat.

Those who are described as intellectuals choose that café, which suits them, compatible with the poverty of their conditions in general. It also relieves them of the severity of isolation or strangeness in a world that does not care about culture or intellectuals, where they are seen as an accessory to the boards of economics, trade, and politics, so that any intellectual is a considered a step, or a staircase, for someone in this or that area.

There is the fancy Groppi Café, where you can remember those great ones who passed through or stayed in it, a renewable trace of its guests, visitors, or residents. It is no secret that every café has its own regulars, and this small group of regulars is intercontinental, common in all cafés, perhaps justified, and provides mutual moral and financial benefits.

The artist, writer, poet, or companion may feel as though they are sitting beside Naguib Mahfouz at an Egyptian café, especially since Mahfouz often frequented cafés. Thus they will feel a kind of kinship to him, and emulation soon turns into a desire to obtain the glories he acquired. The Nobel Prize was his crowning moment, and it is a prize always discussed and analyzed for the reasons, motives, and goals that led to granting it to this or that author. And because Mahfouz is the first and only Arab author to receive the Nobel Prize, he remains in the spotlight, within the reach of arrows that form everything, and at the same time preserves his high literary position within the art field to which he contributed and helped found, where he was its most important pioneer.

The habit of disagreeing about everything is the privilege of the Eastern man. It disturbs his days and obstructs him on his way to understanding.

The intellectual loses his peculiarity and uniqueness. He remains on the lowest rung in the world of consumption because his products are not popular and do not generate direct profit. So he remains a stranger everywhere he goes, and his alienation grows heavy inside him.

The intellectual café, with its misery and dirt, forms a meeting point for a large percentage of displaced Syrians. It is similar in atmosphere to the Sarouja in Damascus, and is slightly closer to the Perfection Café, but different in its service and quality. And because the Syrian feels that he is a temporary resident, there is no harm in him sitting for hours in a place in a terrible state, then going back to where he is staying with a feeling of impermanence.

They go from the coffee shop to the different parts of this city, which is a continent onto itself. To Tahrir Square, to enjoy the view of tents, banners, and some small gatherings that are constantly shrinking. The metro is rightly the greatest achievement in Cairo. That's what I tell myself whenever I take it somewhere: despite what it carries around and the loud and terrifying noise it makes, it's impressive. In the metro, as in other forms of public transportation, the phenomenon of reading the Qur'an or praying is spreading. People do it either with clear and audible mumblings or with swinging movements that set a steady rhythm. And let's not forget the necessary duty of reading the Qur'an!

Sixth of October: It's a city with a certain symbolism, considered modern in the midst of a vast desert, built in a modern style, and enjoying a tidy calm. It has embraced thousands of displaced Syrian families, such that it's become known as the capital of Syrians in Cairo, where the displaced have established schools, homes, and restaurants. Many of them entered the core of working life after a period of waiting and follow-ups that made them feel like temporary residents who were set to return home any day, as soon as a solution to war in their country was found. But they found their stays extended, and temporary became semi-temporary, such that they were forced to search for ways to make money to fund their stay. This was especially true since their savings were dwindling, and what charitable institutions gave was not enough for them to survive. So it became necessary for them to find ways to support themselves and work so they could get rid of the crime of unemployment that had attached itself to them and so they could stop wasting their time lamenting the lives, properties, and money they had lost.

It is difficult for anyone to compete with the Egyptians in their own country, for they suffer from an excess in everything, especially unexploited human power. Still, the Syrians strive to build up the areas where they live and prove their independence.

The diverse Syrian cuisine changes, depending on what neighborhood it's in. Syrian business chains and stores began to emerge, and, in every neighborhood, there is more than one restaurant serving Syrian dishes and products, frequented by those Syrians who don't like the flavors of Egyptian cuisine. Thus they begin to establish a country of their own in the temporary exile, which they are beginning to understand was not as temporary as they had thought.

There are many things the two peoples have in common, but there are also many differences. As much as they are united, they are divided. Friendliness is evident in the Egyptian's celebration of his Syrian brother, and he sympathizes and prays for him. But at the same time, he is busy with himself and his own country's collapse. There are also some who exploit the needs of the displaced and swindle them. The press made headline news of some girls who got married to Egyptian men, exaggerating the story for political gain, and they didn't mention the Syrians who were being used as bait. There are also many cases in which landlords took advantage of the ignorance of refugees and rented them houses for twice the usual cost, and were pleased by their profit.

The displaced person complains about any city he moves to, since he's searching for his home in new cities, after his world has been destroyed. The Syrians ought to read Palestinian literature, as they are the displaced of the new century. The details are somewhat different, but what is coming is the loss of home, family, and homeland.

The Waves of Alexandria

I arrived in Alexandria in the evening. Anti-constitution protesters were blocking the roads, so we had to circle around and enter the city via its darkened side streets, which looked more miserable and dangerous that night because of the rain. Far from the hardships of the road, the noise of the car, the suffocating crisis, and the crowdedness of Cairo, the drive took little time. I drove as fast as I could to the hotel, anxious for the warmth of bed, imagining myself sprawled out, exhausted, on my comfortable bed in the warm room after a hot bath.

People's faces looked tired, the streets were dirty, and the congestion was building up. Contradictory statements covered the walls and the streets, a city that swings between yes and no, between a bright yesterday, a mortgaged present, and a foggy and cloudy tomorrow.

Was I inventing tricks to distract myself from my exile and loneliness?

I paid no attention to the questions and answers that crowded my mind, nor to the speculations that tried to seep in. At times, I resented my own subliminal politicization of many things. I think words spoil the majesty of the situation, and make it lose its charm and glory.

I was so eager to reach the hotel. I quickly crawled into bed and stayed there for a while as things began to calm down outside. I could hear the lulling sound of the sea. Hunger howled tirelessly, and I thought of the importance of having a woman in one's life. I got out of bed and pulled open the curtains. I was surprised by the beautiful scene in front of me and the sudden shift in my emotions. I asked myself whether this was real, or whether I had read it in a novel or watched it in a movie. It occurred to me that the beautiful and enchanting things we see in the cinema and read in novels remain far from us. We dream about them without living them.

The beach of Alexandria, oh, the pleasure of that beach

The beach deceived us, though Alexandria we reached.

I tried very hard to fall asleep but couldn't. I reopened the door to the balcony, which overlooked the sea, and a cold breeze caressed my face. I went back inside, put on my leather jacket, turned on the kettle to make myself a coffee, and went out to sit on the balcony, on an antique wooden chair.

Various dates flooded my memory, and the phenomenal view made my mind wander. Alexandria: a source of wealth for many past poets and artists, a city written about by many historians and novelists. It is a scene of contradictions, a testimony to my visit and my disappointment.

The five-star Palestine Hotel overlooks the sea—with its sleeping boats, flying gulls, and foam embracing the beach. It stirred a mysterious tenderness inside me, and a silent tear slid onto my cheek. I blamed myself for my banality, for I often disturb such lovely moments with the stupidity of bitter remembrance.

The Palestine Hotel stands tall, inside a park with an entrance fee. The park, which was once the gardens of King Farouk, occupies a strategic spot in Alexandria, combining the mountain, the plain, and the sea, giving access to many joys and pleasures. It is an outlet for lovers fleeing the protests and the city's hustle and bustle. They can relax at the park and look out at the sea, overflowing with yearning but content to steal simple touches and kisses in the shade of a rock or tree, or inside a car parked out of sight. Everyone there is considerate of those around them, because they all live in similar conditions. This forms a bond, and overlooking such things is better for everyone.

It made me happy: the sight of lovers in the park's corners, sheltering in the semi-darkness, stealing kisses and interrupted pleasures, peeping at others between one movement and the next. It seemed there was a sense of collaboration among the parkgoers.

I smiled as I said the name Palestine. I thought of how Arabs were obsessed with turning their defeats into victories. After they lost Palestine on the map, they tried to resurrect it in the form of camps or hotels in a number of countries, creating several fictitious "Palestines," while Palestine, the dream, is lost. It's as though they wish to convert it into a trademarked name, so the five-star hotel is a free state with a catchy, unifying moniker. I remember the dirtiest intelligence branch in Syria, which was known as the Palestine branch.

In the morning, the atmosphere was magical. I sat for more than an hour, watching the raging, roaring sea and the foam left behind on the sand after the waves crashed against it and retreated. I saw humanity in the ebb and flow of the sea, or perhaps my memories were imitating it—either way, it's the same. The morning cold shook me out of my anxiety and evening disappointment, the bitter coffee altered my mood. Positivity seeped into my day.

I wanted to get to know the city and explore it on foot. My aspiration of exploring the city was somewhat naïve and overly simplified, for a city like Alexandria covers such a vast area that it is impossible to explore with the ease I'd imagined. Still, I insisted on walking as far as I could. I started down the streets across from the park, dove into it, took mental pictures of the views, read the signs and billboards. The sun was heating up the trees, the walls, and the ground, which was soaked in the previous day's rain. I stopped into a cafe to use the restroom, which was empty except for two workers placing chairs around the tables.

I didn't ask for directions, because I was roaming the city aimlessly. I considered renting a car to visit Alexandria's famous public library, but I immediately gave up on the idea because I wanted to spend this day at a distance from my obsession with books and libraries. I also did not want to waste the opportunity to see a city that I had always dreamt and read about in books that had depicted it as great, amazing, wonderful.

I was startled by the snarled traffic that seemed to be on the rise. The waiter laughed at my reaction and noted that there were only a few traffic lights in all of Alexandria. That was upsetting to hear, for I did not want to compare it to Tokyo, which is said to have removed all their traffic lights, having done so after paving the roads and building new bridges in an attempt to eliminate the traffic problem.

I stopped at a cafe by the beach to have a cup of coffee and rest. The nice thing about Alexandria is that it's easy to get to the beach from anywhere. Despite the neglect that is no less marked than in other parts of Egypt, it still shows its greatness in the face of history and the present.

In my mind, Alexandria is associated with art, history, and beauty.

I consider art to be sacred, and that no sacred elements can shackle it. Art is created by a human being. It is the epitome of humanity. This is how I dream of it, and when I see people place the sanctity of a historical figure above the right to question and debate, I rush to find a way art can provoke discussion of any topic or thought, to deal with it and look into the background of any protected figure.

Each historical period has its own soul, its good and bad qualities. So I don't understand why, when I search for the spirit of our current time, I see a corpse among the rubble of frivolous people eager to flaunt it. What might the spirit of our time be? The spirit of blood? Revenge? Refuge? Displacement? The spirit of loss? The incinerators? Or are we living in an era without a soul? Who is the unknown person who will save us and protect future generations from the miseries we have created?

Each historical period has its own soul, and every age has its sacred fire. Every person also has his own time, his own holy fire.

While at the beach, I recalled a conversation I'd had with a friend who is fanatic about her Phoenician roots. She told me, "I am Ugaritic; I take pride in my Phoenician roots. I carry my ancient history in my heart, in my soul and in my practices. Here, the sea is open to history. I build on its myths, and it carries me into the future. We were tied up in a miserable nationalism, and they traded in it. We have nothing but the lineage of Phoenicians to keep us firmly rooted in this land, and that eases their falsehood and hypocrisy and helps preserve their trade and privileges."

I did not ask her to clarify or explain. She chose to discuss this topic and to condemn everyone. She was trying to express her view of the collapse of grassroots, and even national projects that had been aborted. She called for the necessity of returning to history in order to extract its pearls and remove the veil from its greatness.

A combination of factors that have been present, but sublimated, have now become a burning fire, a bullet that kills, and a rich joke. It is amazing how the shrapnel of spoken words can fight fierce wars in our minds and destroy human life.

She said, "I am honest about my fanaticism, and I realize that you carry your own fanaticism in your heart and soul. And despite your attempts to downplay, sugarcoat, and even embellish the current situation, it remains clear, and I see that plainly in you, especially when I press you on it or question your history, the nobility of your people, and your dream."

I went along with her, pointing out that she was being tyrannical with her opinions and views, to which she replied that those who aren't are the helpless ones! She supports her view with poems and proverbs from modern history, but she sifts through and chooses what suits her to add it to her heritage, and she accumulates things along the way to make up her historic heaven.

She saw in me a reflection of her oppressed history and another face to the setbacks that our tyrannical regimes have piled upon us. She told me that revolutions reveal people's nakedness, and that this revolution exposed everyone's. She said, "They set us back hundreds of years. They took us back to a period that's convenient for them and decided that we would live in that bloody era. But I chose instead to move away from the era of fighting and destruction and into the era of construction and civilization."

Sometimes I ask myself, honestly, whether all this bloodshed was necessary for us to be able to start a new tomorrow. But they left us no choice. They left people with two methods of killing, and each one ultimately led to the other. I have no doubt that we are headed into a dark age. For my part, I believe our salvation will come by returning to the time before the quarrels, which have only led to more destruction and bloodshed.

I remember her pain when she told me, "Oh, if only we could go back to the time before all this misfortune, we would've been great. I inhabit an imagined kingdom, rebuilt by my imagination and passion. I'll make it come to life in others, too, and I'll dedicate myself to reviving it. History is repeating itself, and it's bloody and vulgar. This is the cycle it goes through, but I'll interrupt it. I'll repair the wheels of history and I will take the wheel. I know that I'm only a faint voice in the clamor of the growing violence, but I'm a steadfast, confident believer. Belief in something keeps it alive. Here, I now see pillars on the rise.

"There is no civilization without destruction and blood." With this sentence, she concluded her theory and her justification for her increasing fanaticism.

And with that sentence ringing in my ears, I went back to discovering Alexandria, and to getting to know my part in the great city.

Bridges

"Blessed is he who calls me Turkish."

A billboard bearing this expression greets you at the Istanbul Airport. Your memory is suddenly thrown into years of oppression, humiliation, and delusion. What does it mean to say that you're Turkish? And why do you expect to receive happiness with this declaration? You imagine this heavenly earth has been blessed in your name. I recall the names of some of those whose boasting of their Turkish identity brought them no peace, and I remember my little shepherd friend, who was killed by a Turkish soldier. Perhaps this slogan—engraved in the guard's mind—blinded him and led him to kill a child and terrorize an entire city.

I realize that the nationalists want to hide their illusions of Sultanism and consolidate their hegemony under the guise of a modern approach, in keeping with the times. They seek to melt others in their fires and expel them from the custody of their ideologies and thoughts, instead sending them out into the world of modernity, power, and the future. Such mottos made up the bridge that connected them with their dreams.

For someone to say, "I am Turkish," and to brag about it, means they are already belittling the identities of others. This verbal affiliation presupposes another, fiercer affiliation that excludes any other stance that might contradict it. Dissociation is thus the starting point for acceptable engagement and desired integration.

Yet the bliss that this slogan suggests is disrupted, as whoever strives to assume other nationalities remains stamped with the seal of his previous affiliation. That is, some Turks will remain of Kurdish or Arab origins. Many overstate their chauvinism and hostility to their own kin in their vigorous pursuit of new nationalities and faiths. This is a habit that many have fallen victim to in this region. You see them proud of their nationalities, as though they had a blessed status. They grant them holiness in order to strengthen their positions. And any person who fancies himself loyal because of this belonging has found himself there by chance.

The East is full of illusions that masterfully turn lies into legends.

Istanbul today appears caught between its affiliations. It is made up of many cities, and it is a world in one city, or the city of the world. A bridge between continents and civilizations. A city of dialogues and clashes. In it, opposites converge and compose different, strange paintings. In it, history sits on your chest and pokes its head around every corner. History governs relationships, draws proximity and distance, and organizes visions and plans. Many have flirted with Istanbul, adored and written about it. Each person clothes the city in a different fashion, preserves it in a unique way and with striking presence.

In Istanbul, there are no narrow affiliations, and circles and affiliations overlap. Openness is its hallmark. It's as if the city's rich geography and entrances and exits cast a shadow over its people and inhabitants, imprinting them with a special, distinctive character. Its name bears the burdens of history and the future for its people. It belongs to the West and the East. The West and East are its own, and no generalizations apply. What is true of others may not be true of this city.

In Istanbul, everyone finds their private city. It appears to them a legend among cities and civilizations, at the height of beauty, luxury, and progressiveness. Spirits cannot rest in it, and souls cannot stand still. The waters of its bays and seas constantly purify it. This is how the lovers of Istanbul would describe her.

And since everyone sees in Istanbul their own city, and since I have my share of every city I've passed through or lived in, I feel I own my own share of Istanbul as well. My Istanbul was unique in its historical monuments, museums, and its embrace of seasons, times, beauty, and grace. I raise the slogan, "We are blessed with Istanbul."

After I left the hotel on Taksim Street, I smiled as I repeated that name: *taksim,* or division. It is customary for the squares and streets to be named after slogans of unity, freedom, or some other catchy phrase, but it's strange for the most famous square in Istanbul to be named after "division." This raises questions. Perhaps this is a sign of the city's many paradoxes and oddities. Apart from what is meant by the city's name and its roots, its contemporary references and connotations dominate the historical image of the city.

There, I met a charming girl. Her beauty was such that it "would make you cry or land you in prison," as some young men would say. Her hair was black, her skin clear, her body blessed with well-proportioned curves. I spoke to her in broken English. She asked me about my country, and she looked happy when I told her I was from Damascus. So she attempted to speak to me in an understandable Arabic, but quickly went quiet when I told her that I was originally from the Kurdish regions. I asked her if she knew any Kurds, or if she knew anything about them, to which she groaned and sighed. I tried to get her to talk more, but it was clear that she wanted to be rid of the burden of questions and the weight of answers.

I remember a bachelor friend who was looking for his lost love. He told me that only a woman could bring charm to a city, and that a city without women was dull, cold, and hollow. When a woman appears, she brings joy, pleasure, and ecstasy. When you say the name of a city, and end it with a full stop, know that the city lacks soul. For you must have a woman in every city. Find or invent one! For to live in a strange city without a woman is to live in destructive alienation. A woman dispels those feelings of estrangement.

I went to the Gulf and looked at the royal palaces from afar. They are like Alexandria Park in their prestige and appearance, and in the way they sit on a throne of breathtaking magic. My heart felt full. I reminded myself that the descendants of Muhammad Ali Pasha had ruled Egypt, and before them, Saladin. I remembered the theory popular among the Kurds that Muhammad Ali Pasha was of Kurdish origins and was a commander in the Ottoman army. Besides this bit of information, other details seemed to bring together Kurds and the history of Muhammad Ali and his dynasty. As for the Kurdish origins of Saladin, only those who are plagued with the Ba'athist disease doubt it. The school curriculum in Syria labels him an Arab leader. They actually think falsifying information in a school textbook will rewrite historical facts! I am not going to analyze the personality of Saladin and his historical role. I only note this popular theory about him.

After I discovered this lie in school textbooks, I became suspicious of every part of the school curriculum, especially the history books that were riddled with forgeries, fabrications, and lies. I asked myself how much work would be needed to fill the gaps in people's memories and correct the misinformation that the system had spread in their minds, in order to convince them that such lies were truths. In addition to history books, there are "national education" books, which are utterly disgusting and repulsive, as they include twisted illusions and sicknesses that reflect reality's emptiness.

As I sat on the Gulf Corniche, enjoying the waves that struck the concrete wall a few steps away, I felt as though I were sitting on Khalid Lake Corniche in Sharjah. I noticed that Sharjah echoes Istanbul in the designs of its coastal mosques. The domes are luminous, adding beauty to the lake, and in turn absorbing the lake's beauty and glory. The mosques face one another, adding the finishing touches to a complete painting. The mosques circle a gulf that longs for its royal heritage.

There, I am forever accompanied by imagination. I remember Yilmaz Guney and his short life full of accomplishments. Among the many Turkish writers whose books and novels I have read, Guney's writing sticks in my mind the most. I find strength in every corner I pass. This legendary director's life took many turns, and he faced impossible challenges that another man would have needed two lifetimes to overcome. He was a volcano of a man. He achieved what institutions were unable to at the time.

Every time I move to a new city, I weep for mine. I weep for my dreams, distorted in my exile. I weep for the lines drawn on the world map.

In Istanbul, there are millions of Kurds. I walked its old streets like a child looking into a mirror in the city market in Aleppo with its stones paving the road, its alleys, its streets and shops. Everything in these markets mimics the old markets of Aleppo, and the neighboring streets remind me of Souk Al-Hamidiye in Damascus.

I recalled how the sultans brought engineers and architects to their city from all parts of the Sultanate. How they wanted to build a city that combined the various aesthetics of their dispersed Sultanate, so that it would be distinguished by its uniqueness and bear witness to their ingenuity and history.

As I wandered around, I contemplated what was and what might have been. I saw a girl next to her crippled father. That is, because of their age difference, I assumed it was her father. She played a sad melody on her flute. I stood nearby enjoying her music, the beauty of which made me forget the pain of the scene in front of me. I sat down on a bench, since I had time to spare, and I continued listening to her play. They probably thought I was some strange tourist. They seemed used to that sort of thing.

I gave them some money, and the girl took the opportunity to rest a little. She laid the flute on her lap, as though it were her newborn, and sat there in silence. Her father gave me a look that told me that his daughter would not be playing again for some time, but I wasn't too shy to stick around, so I took out my map to get a better idea of where I was.

Soon the girl asked her father, in sweet-sounding Kurdish, if they could go home. He replied that they would in about an hour. He told her that he had collected a decent amount of money for the day, but that he was not able to count it because there was a tourist nearby who hadn't left yet. I didn't want to interrupt their intimate chitchat and felt guilty for eavesdropping on them, since they didn't know I could understand what they were saying. But, at the same time, I saw in this an opportunity to get to know them a little without embarrassing them or myself.

I wanted to speak to them in Kurdish, since I missed having conversations in Kurdish. I felt the words flow from my lips, and in order not to look at their embarrassed expressions once they realized that I'd understood their conversation, I picked up my phone and pretended to be distracted by my map: "Where are you from, Uncle...?"

They were surprised to hear my question in a Kurdish very close to theirs. They looked a little disturbed, even. But the man quickly recovered and took the initiative to answer.

From the village of Batman.

Your daughter plays beautifully.

Thank you. Where are you from, Cousin?

From Syria, Uncle... from Amuda.

Welcome. May God help you. You are reclaiming a life we lived and suffered, and you continue to pay the penalty until this day. How is it going over there now?

Fine...

I said it as a matter of habit, but I didn't truly mean it.

What 'fine,' brother? I see the war grinding you down, and those fleeing it are drowning in the depths of this dark sea. A few days ago, a boat with dozens of you sank. How I suffered for them. Young men in their prime, fleeing to Europe, dreaming of salvation, devoured by the sea monster. I swear I cried for them, and I still cry every time I remember them. It's as if we were destined to be the fuel that others burn in their wars. We pay the fees with the souls of our young and the future of our children. Those poor people thought they were on the threshold of heaven, but the raging sea-ghoul was lurking around them, and they became food for the predators and monsters. I do not deny that human beings have vanquished the beasts of land and sea with their brutality and savagery, but no one sees or wants to deal with the unsolvable problems. Instead, they pour more gasoline on the fire... I cry for them as I cry for my house, my village, and my children. It seems the curse of massacres will never leave us. I remember more than half a century ago, we heard that a cinema was burned in the town of Amuda. It was a fiery massacre that killed hundreds, and it remains unsolved. And then, only a few days ago, this massacre in the sea plunged our hearts into sadness and grief and added to our oppression, dispersal, and accumulated loss.

It's as if the fate of that city is to offer its people as sacrifices, to satisfy the stalking ghoul of death. Between burning and drowning, its history is lost, its children wasted. Many reasons and excuses were given for this horrific incident, each holding another party responsible. But none of that matters anymore—not after all that devastation.

Every day, I watch thousands of people. This city is a way station for people as they travel to and from other places. I sit with my daughter and stay with her against my will. I cannot go back to my village. I heard that they began to rebuild it after they burned it down, along with about four thousand other villages like it. They try to lure people back, but how can we go back, and what do we go back to? My land was turned into a military barracks, so should I go back to my village as a beggar? Listen to me, Cousin, diaspora can be a curtain and a veil. Here, we can provide for ourselves, and we have grown accustomed to our lifestyle. Only my daughter, who is my consolation in this world, did not break my back or my heart. Sometimes I think about her fate, especially since I am on the threshold of death. I am tempted to toss her in this bay as food for whales, God forgive me and my dark thoughts. But then, other times, I wish she and I were on that sinking boat together in place of those children who drowned. Life after your children have died is a raging hell. The fires of my heart cannot be extinguished, my pain grows, and I relive my loss every day. When I see children and young people their age, I feel their presence in this life. I imagine their children and wives with me in one big house, frolicking and having fun.

I moved closer, hoping the proximity would ease my pain and sadness, and hoping to hear him better since he had subconsciously lowered his voice. Sadness engulfed him and forced him to settle down. I did not want to interrupt his train of thought or speech, but when I realized that his silence would be a long one, I asked about his village and the reason he had been forced to leave.

He looked grieved as he answered. "Oh my brother, this world is a constant test. I was the mayor of the village when the battles intensified between the Turkish army and the Kurdish youth in the mountains. The Turks wanted me to inform them about any suspicious movements. They tried to bribe me at first, then to terrorize me. They took turns trying to tempt and intimidate me. They promised me land, status, and favors in exchange for telling them all the details, infiltrating the organization, and helping them capture our young men. I refused, although I had many reservations about what the young people were doing. But I was not willing to cooperate with the Turks or to sell out my own blood for cheap. They did not accept that anyone could remain neutral in a raging war. On a day when a number of young men in the village were resting and planning to leave at nightfall, they surprised us with rockets and bombs, which fell on us from all sides. They burned everything to the ground and destroyed the village. It was a hideous massacre. Those who escaped were tortured because they refused to reveal the identities of those who died in the massacre. The village was burned down—even our only mosque was not spared. They put all us survivors in a truck and threw us into cities after days of travel. And, as you can see, here we are, ruminating on our pain, carrying our homeland with us, and weeping for our today and tomorrow. This daughter here was my youngest. My three older sons were killed in the bombing. I lost all of them, and I lost my leg, too. Now my daughter and I help one another and complete each other. I remember many jokes about the tragedies of the disabled, and all of them apply to me with my bitterness, misery, and grief. We have no choice. We either survive or die of hunger."

Do you never want to go back, Uncle?

Go back? This heartbreak burns my soul, my son. Maybe I'll ask that my body be sent back, to be buried in the earth of my village beside my sons. But that would be another impossible dream.

It seems that refugees' dreams, wherever they find themselves, transform into pain, a constant reminder of their permanent diaspora.

The Road to Hawler

I had a conversation with some friends from Istanbul's literary and community. They were debating whether it was a good idea to invest in Iraqi Kurdistan. It made me think of an artist friend who had told me she was seriously considering investing her name, her art, and her drama career in Erbil, because she had heard that they celebrate the Arabs who seek them out.

She told me, sarcastically, "Maybe they want to show us their brotherhood, partnership, closeness, and sense of duty toward us. Or maybe this is their way of paying us back for what we've done to them, whether directly or indirectly. Regardless of whether we were active participants in their oppression or silent observers to the crimes committed against them over the decades."

She said the opportunity had come to woo them and reap the fruits of their economic prosperity, especially since their region enjoyed safety, comfort, and stability, and was now a destination for investors from neighboring countries. She told me that she had learned that great artists had founded production companies there, which had paved the way for their futures.

She said, with a malicious laugh, "I can use my feminine wiles to pave the way for my own private company. I'm okay with one of the nouveau riche partnering with me. In fact, I need their partnership. I believe some of them need ways to launder their money, and I need money to clean my days and secure my future. So it's a partnership to benefit all parties."

She told me what a friend of hers had told her about Kurds: how they were a people who went overboard for strangers, and how that was their weakness, which was sometimes used to insult them. It caused me a lot of bitterness and heartache to hear it often repeated that Kurds would sell out themselves and their brothers, and that they would go to extremes in order to harm each other. I remembered certain moments in history when Kurds had stood by others, when the others had not meet them in turn, as brothers would. In recent times, others had begun to exploit them, as though they were a tool to be used to strengthen their influence in the region.

She added, "What matters to me is to share peace and security, and to be able to rebuild my life. I'll achieve my dreams of making it into cinema, and I'll use their goal of luring Arab partners. It will be an equal and transparent partnership on all sides."

She scolded me for my excessive idealism when it came to my ideal homeland. She told me that reality promised otherwise. She saw me as a Don Quixote in my struggle with my idealistic dreams, and she believed that the ghoul of reality would gobble up those fantasies. I am unwilling to agree with her belief that the economy is the blood of our times and its spirit comes through projects and investments. I refuse to be convinced that the backbone of future development is not literature, art, education, or science as I had previously imagined, but that instead money is the master of this wild era.

She tried to calm me down so that maybe I would be able to look at the place with an impartial gaze. She tried to persuade me to take the city as a stable place to work and overlook the facets of aborted dreams that tire us out, that seem to have been destroyed and cannot be rebuilt. She felt that we are merely on our journey to reconstruction, looking for a safe haven for our future.

She expressed her plan to infiltrate the heart of the city's velvet community. She said, "An interview with this or that channel, and a little support for the cause, a bit of praise and admiration for local authorities, and giving a unique perspective on energy and power would put me in the spotlight and draw attention. I'd make sure to broadcast my secret messages between the lines of every speech I make. The brief time I've spent with these politicians has given me a knack for acting, the likes of which I could never have gotten during my years as a professional. The scenes are edited to produce more persuasive political films. There, I'll be able to combine both my sides: my professionalism in acting and what I have gained of political skills. I'll arm myself with it to fool politicians. They're the ones who used to say that they had no friends other than the mountains, and yet here they are, easily swayed when a foreign intellectual, thinker, or artist praises them, celebrates them, or brags about their friendship and history. It would be easy for me to make it into their circles with my investments and projects."

She added, "I can benefit from the tens of thousands brought here by circumstance. They'll form an army of innocent actors who can be employed in some of the projects that I intend to present. As a friend told me, there are many who suffer in the worst conditions. I can't forget his tears as he told me how there are hundreds who went to bed hungry at a time when they could be imprisoned for years and severely tortured as punishment for uttering *his* name. Those who defected, the escapees, and the refugees have changed the country's demographics and contributed to a revitalization of social mobility. I like his righteousness, and I see the essence behind what he's saying."

It seems the Syrian Kurds have been more successful than the other millions of Kurds in other regions, and they are always the ones being sacrificed for others, in the name of their brothers and sisters. But when the Syrian Kurds have needed help, the others forget their sacrifices and reject them. Some have even treated them as strangers and refugees. Imagine a person being treated as a strange refugee among his family, after he had put his money and comfort on the line to defend them. Many dreamed of finding refuge there, but instead what awaited them was a planned exodus.

When our conversation grew heated, I told her about my tragedy, trauma, and misfortune. My eyes welled up with tears when she said, "Life is a never-ending camp, my friend. As you yourself keep repeating, this world is a black market. Experience will teach them a lot, as they're on the cusp of entering the world of competition and power. Complacency, underestimation, and force will not help them."

Coincidence becomes a habit among friends. In fact, it is more beautiful than novels and art in opening up the strange and unexpected.

This friend of mine insisted that I accompany her to Hawler, but I refused. It pains me that some treat the Syrian Kurds in Hawler as strangers, or see them as suspicious, and that the displaced human group there is seen as a Syrian-Kurdish community.

"The Kurdish community in Kurdistan" is a depressing expression that betrays memory and imprisons the future.

I told her about some of my obsessions and fears. I told her that she would do well and be welcomed, and that she would quickly rise into the spotlight, especially since her artistic presence was dedicated to souls and memories. And I did not hide the fact that there were many officials who had grown addicted to the cruelty of the mountains and that her kindness would please them.

I am not surprised by the behavior of some Kurdish men. I'm referring to the type of man who would be classified as having an advanced case of eastern fanaticism. He would, you see, adore a liberated woman and sacrifice a lot for her companionship and time. But he would also swing into a cranky and serious mood when he was at home with his woman. He would be keen to preserve his prestige at home while presenting himself as frivolous, lighthearted, and civilized outside it.

I tell her that humans are actors by nature, and that they will remain actors to the end. The difference between her and the rest of us is that she is paid money for her acting, while we pay a heavy tax for ours, taxes reaped in the years of our short lives.

Is reality the mirror of art, or is it the opposite? It doesn't matter, since the result is that they both reflect one another. I am surprised by her absolute ignorance of us, but at the same time I am not really surprised. She is busy with herself, her body, her beauty and grace, and like everyone who falls into the trap of the spotlight and fame, she is blinded by lights that prevent her from seeing other dimensions.

I see that she is happy with her discovery, dreaming of a renewed glory and of breathing life into her future project. Partnership with her would represent a new kind of unity. Economy is the basis of the future, and the foundation for understanding and love. I recognize her goals in establishing this partnership: they are to revive her name in the field and modernize it. It's okay—she'll make money, and they'll have fun in a bright and hopeful future.

Pleasure is bought and sold. Everything is bought and sold; even a person is bought and sold there, as in many other places, and this is what is so dangerous. The cause for which millions sacrificed, the dream that ate up so many lives, has become for some the capital that makes them lose their memory. The greatest danger is amnesia, for memory is the spirit of the times, and it lives in independent human beings.

Reality is shocking. And one of the truest things ever written is that reality will always be a human sword. When the poet Abu Tammam began his epic by saying that the sword is more truthful than literature, he was aware of the limits he was drawing, crossing, and imposing on reality. In turn, he drew a new, different reality that corresponds to its own intensity and strength.

This woman wanted me to be her adviser on all things Kurdish because, every time we spoke, she learned something new from me. She said that, through me, she had been introduced to a history of oppression and sadness.

I told her that the great calamity was that everyone was trying to exploit us as cards to be dealt. They wanted us to be subject to their policies, decisions, interests, and influence. They didn't realize that we will not accept being used as tools of pressure, blackmail, or as a stage for their accountability. These mountains, which provide us with neutrality and freedom, also protect us from ourselves.

I spoke to her about the critical stages that brothers went through when they exchanged the venom of fierce and deadly hostility in Kurdistan, and I didn't hide the conflicts that are still raging between different social, political, and linguistic divisions. Nor did I hide the spread of tribal and clan divisions. What is most terrible there, however, is the continued practice of female circumcision and the high rate of suicide among women. I told her that many do not want to be reminded of the dark days that followed the massacres committed by the buried tyrant against our brothers there, nor of the dark events that continue to take place from time to time. It's as though not discussing them will erase them or make it as though they never happened.

She always corrects herself when she says North Iraq: "I mean Kurdistan." Then she begs my pardon in her beautiful way.

I do not know how to communicate to her about the difficult situations through which we have lived that we cannot explain. I found no need to tell her that a Kurd quickly pardons the other, while keeping the embers of grief alive in his heart. He is always willing and ready to be a sword for others and a spearhead in any battle. Yet to himself, he remains his own enemy.

Isn't the symbol of the Kurdish people the partridge, which is known for attacking its own kind?

Kurds like to feel as though history is reprimanding them for building up the glories of others under various names and slogans, while neglecting to make their own, independent history. So it's easy to see the overlapping, broken, and patched-up history that echoes reality and its projections.

We find ourselves facing a difficult situation: the problem of history and its curses, which haunt us. When forced to come face to face with ourselves and others, we realize that we were the fuel in battles that others fought, as well as the lost currency wasted on them. Our blood was the cheapest.

She wanted me to be flexible and realistic so that I could keep pace with these modern, progressive times. She was right to suggest it, but I could not pretend to be that, not when the matter involves us Kurds. She wanted me to give up the dreams of the mountains, to cross the threshold of the stock exchanges and enter the snake's hole.

Corporations are the haunts of reality and the future. Only femininity can tame fierce human monsters. This was how she described reality, and I agreed with her to a large extent. But how will I be able to tame the revolution that is sweeping through me, keeping me dormant in the camps of grief, misery, and oppression, while there are aggressive trade deals being made at the expense of my grief and misery?

She reminds me of something I used to repeat to her: "These times are not what they had imagined. The wind flows by the will of the navigator, and the current is overpowered by the ship." One of our teachers of Arabic literature used to repeat that to us in school. I remember what I used to tell her when we spoke about mountains and their symbolism in people's hearts and souls. I would tell her that I believed that the waters of the seas, no matter how much it flooded, burned, or fell, would not submerge the mountain peaks. I live inside my illusions and idealism, but I will try to reconcile them with the reality that preys on both dreams and illusions.

Erbil, as she said, and Howler, as I corrected her with a laugh, would be a new destination. The glitter and shine of oil would deepen the bonds of brotherhood with partners and neighbors. But words of hate are on the rise here and there... God help us!

The Meeting of Nations

I went to a Latin dance party after being invited by a South American friend. Well, I thought it was a Latin dance party, at first, but it became clear when I got there that it was a simple dance practice session and nothing more. I locked eyes with some Syrian and Arab women, who were trying to get in some practice dancing. Then as soon as I crossed the threshold and headed toward the hall that had been loaned out by one of the churches, I turned on my heels and went back outside, telling my friend that I had thought it was an invitation to a party and not a dance class.

My friend, the dance instructor, tried to get me to stay by telling me that the trainees would perform a dance at the end of class, but I insisted on leaving and told her that I might come back later. I didn't want to embarrass the Syrian and Arab women there, as they tried to tame their bodies and train them to dance in the Latin way. I did not want to ruin their joy at taking part in an erotic dance that they would never have been allowed to learn in their countries.

There were a few men in the hall. I knew one of them, and he urgently called out to me to join them. He didn't understand the sensitivity of the situation for these women, and how my presence would be a constraint for them. He behaved in a spontaneous manner that I consider the enemy of many people who fled our Eastern societies, as it forced them to act, borrow, conceal, and hide.

I didn't think much about the presence of other men in the hall, studying dance alongside the women and girls, but it could be an embarrassment to some I knew. A stranger will always remain a stranger, and he will not explore the secrets of a person's history or his cultural, intellectual, social, and religious background. But he will be a person who feels embarrassed in front of those who know him, not those in the room with him, and he will present himself in his new character that he tries to embody, highlight, and project.

I can analyze the look of confidence, misery, grief, disappointment, shock, and the curses in the eyes of the women I encountered in the dance lesson that I did not attend. The mere sight of me was enough to disturb them, to send them back to the social shell they were trying to overcome, the obstacles and delusional lines that still exerted a strong influence over them and over their lives in this refuge.

If a stranger were to see the swaying body of one of these women, he would not look beyond the movements; he would not see that what was veiled had finally become free, that it was permitted exposure after such a long concealment. And he would not know anyone from the social milieu to which the group belongs, and so his gossip or talk about a woman and her dancing would not cause her any harm. The matter would not go beyond the dance floor, and it would not require any justifications that would make it a constant headache for her. As for me—and I do not mean me personally, but rather what I represent as an individual—I am a part of the society to which she belongs and is often present in. I may cause her, from her point of view, embarrassment with any potential gossip that bitter tongues may spread, or any damage her reputation may receive from false accusations.

I wonder why the existence of one of us is embarrassing for the other in times of supposed happiness, during one's favorite pastimes. Why is the refugee a wolf to other refugees, keeping them captive to previous judgments that they bear as burdens that cannot be shed?

I wonder about the well of secrets that the stranger represents to each of us, and how he is a welcome presence at times, when a relative would put us on the road to slander, to reliving the past and obscuring memory. I wonder at how diaspora makes a stranger both distant and close at times when it is increasingly important to reconcile the body with the self, to break free from the paranoia that the refugee carries within him and which at times grows exaggerated.

So I left, even though I enjoy watching people dance and find dancing very pleasurable. In fact, I wrote a chapter called "Novel and Dance" in my book *Novel and Life*, in which I pointed out certain aspects of my love for dancing and how it shapes an independent identity for a person. And although I don't know how to dance, I still enjoy watching it. My thoughts took me to situations that I had been through or witnessed. I remembered a friend who used to go to the pool early in the morning, at a time when there were no refugees around who knew her. There was nothing wrong with men seeing her body in a swimsuit then...

I also remembered a Muslim Arab friend of mine who dated a Muslim Arab girl from a small English town. It was so difficult to plan dates with her, since she was afraid to go to his house, but she also wouldn't let him go to hers. Their relationship was in its infancy, and it ended soon after, because of the many obstacles that faced them. Their relationship could not develop into love, since they couldn't even find a spot to have a date. Cafés are acceptable places to meet for Arab and Muslim communities, but still someone could recognize her there, and they might spread rumors about them, which would pave the way for others to exaggerate and gossip about their closeness. Then her reputation would be damaged, and she could get harassed or assaulted as a result, since she was the kind of girl who had no problem meeting up with boys in public places... Bars were also a problem for his girlfriend, because she wore a hijab, and if some drunk or curious person were to take her picture and post it somewhere, she would be responsible for damaging the reputation of all veiled Muslim women. The list of things they had to take into consideration grew, which caused their relationship to lose its value and meaning, so they grew apart and slowly lost touch, virtually, as though they lived on two different, distant, continents.

The eye contact I had with some of them at the threshold of the hall, before I even stepped inside, summarized all those miserable thoughts, conditions, and states that we had inherited, and which we'd brought with us into our new world. It is almost impossible to free ourselves from the past and from our memories. The refugee is a wolf to other refugees, lying in wait for him in the places he least expects, accidentally running into him and disturbing the mood of moments he had worked hard to plan.

The embarrassment that some refugees inflict upon themselves is often repeated when they meet at the Sunday Market, a popular market in Edinburgh where people sell used goods at low prices. Many of the city's residents frequent that market, whether they are Europeans, immigrants, or refugees from different nationalities, so in a way the market is a meeting of nations and represents the whole world, where different cultures, shapes, and colors meet.

When Syrians meet there, they try to hide their embarrassment and keep their gaze lowered so as not to make eye contact with others. If their eyes do meet, they greet each other quickly and shyly, then go on their way as though they live in different worlds, or as though they hardly know each other.

An attempt to explain this phenomenon—which is represented by the apprehension, suspicion, and skepticism that is widespread among refugees from the same country—one would have to look at the contradictory split lives that refugees lead. They claim to rise above certain practices and action, when in reality they are guilty of them. And this is how they remain prisoners of their own delusions and contradictions, which distract them from themselves and their surroundings and exacerbate the alienation within them even more.

Many refugees live in a quagmire of deprivation. They deprive themselves of the charms of the place they inhabit, or their new culture and its uniqueness and distinction. They close themselves off and become afraid of communicating with others and becoming part of society. They fall prey to their suspicion of others and their distrust of themselves, and in return become a walking contradiction when they speak to their families and friends back home. They boast of their presence in their shelters, and they enjoy the flattery and looks of veneration, the pride and envy in the eyes of many back there.

Lone Wolves

Lone wolves, or lost wolves, is an expression that sounds like an exciting literary title. In reality, however, the media uses it to refer to the lone terrorists who run freely, enjoying the world and planning their acts of terror alone or in coordination with the terrorist groups that finance them. They are the spark that detonates the powder keg that is set up to destroy everything and everyone around it.

It is both sad and ironic for such a narrowminded view to spread in societies hosting refugees, among those who suddenly find themselves confronted with their fears. They have tried to locate these fears, which for some have turned into phobias, in the images and faces they encounter. It's as though they have to take a miserable and difficult daily test. They could begin to look at the refugee among them as a lone, lost wolf who can turn on them or kill them at any moment; all he is waiting for is the right opportunity to pounce. They may even go overboard with their suspicions and generalize the image portrayed in the extremist media, which is presented to them as seeds of terrorism that are growing in their environment and world.

I remember the story "Blind," by the Argentine Eduardo Galeano (1940-2015), from his book *The Hunter of Stories*. In it, he relates the Europeans' previous vision of Latin America, and how they used to have irrational prejudices wholly disconnected from history, science, and humanity. He wonders at how Europeans must have seen them in the sixteenth century, then answers that they saw America through the eyes of Theodor de Bry. He describes him as an artist from Liège, who had never been to America, and who was the first to paint the inhabitants of the New World. He notes that his excavations were a graphic translation of the invaders' chronicles.

He confirms that, as de Bry's images show, the meat of European invaders grilling on the coals was the favorite dish of the American cannibals. Then he regrets that miserable image presented on the dish of deceit and deception, exposing the lie of Theodor de Bry, his racist vision, and those who came after him who adopted it: "Pardon the bother, but were those people hungering for human flesh really Indians? In de Bry's engravings, all of them are bald. In America, not a single Indian was bald."

Today, some people have adopted false allegations that refugees carry terrorism in their hearts and souls, and that they could begin plotting their supposed terrorist operations any day. This is a preemptive restriction for the refugees and a surprising criminalization based on speculations and presumptions of their cultural, social, and religious backgrounds.

Perhaps there is an unconscious endeavor to transform today's refugees into contemporary Indians scattered around the globe, dragging their sins behind them, those sins that are the result of tyrannical regimes and their sponsors in the West. They are called a direct cause of the world's strife, and thus the media turns the victim into an executioner, putting the weight on them to capture the supposed wolves before they grow any stronger.

In Britain, residential neighborhoods are spreading and expanding along the margins of British cities, especially the major ones. Some Muslims are confined to ghettoized clusters, creating their space in a land some allege is impure, full of inhabitants who do not fear God and live as atheists. They find themselves the strangers of their time, the preachers who have a responsibility to evangelize while living in their chronic estrangement and alienation, their freedom stolen by the countries that expelled them.

What is surprising is those who live in enclosed bubbles and broadcast speech filled with hatred for society, those who feel superior to their neighbors, who would describe them as lost souls. They would begin preparations for an environment that nurtures young wolves and fills their minds with toxins.

I have no doubt that liberating these people from their closed bubbles and lost ways requires an intellectual revolution that would save them from themselves and their growing evils. This would push them to fall back on their humanity and openness instead of their reticence, illusions, and fear of themselves and others.

Asylum freed me from many illusions that had haunted my imagination and my past thinking, including illusions of what was going on with my world in the East, and others about the world that I had reached in the West, and the strings that linked the two worlds and formed bridges of communication and interaction between them. These include what was being said about the revolution and the sacrifices people made, about belonging to a nation or nationality.

A revolution does not end, and it does not die. Revolutionaries may become martyrs, and other revolutionaries may change into merchants, and those near and far may conspire against it, but it will always remain a revolution against tyranny and criminality. This is the revolution of man in his search for desired freedom. There is no doubt that our revolution was transformed into a comprehensive war against the Syrian people, in which the regime held the country hostage to the restrictions of multiple occupations—Iran, Russia, and the United States—costing the Syrian people immeasurable sacrifices and losses, whether from the side of martyrs, or from the people deformed by the war, psychologically and physically, or in terms of those destroyed cities that will take decades to restore or rebuild. But freedom deserves the efforts being made on its behalf, because reliance on the injustice of bastards would keep the country hostage to destruction for centuries and centuries. Future generations will not tolerate those who surrender to the shame of tyranny.

In the context of wolves, lycanthropy, and going astray, the refugee-writer, or the writer-refugee, is seen by some as a lone wolf. And accordingly, if he were to criticize his new or old societies, then he is referred to by his critics as nothing but an opportunistic writer, hiding in the deceptive gray area that separates belonging to one place and alienation from another, playing with words and contradictions. And if he were to criticize an opportunistic and outward-looking novelist, then he would be accused of being jealous of his success and fame, which shows in his relationships and connections to a corrupt milieu, especially in the system of corruption that laid the foundations for many swamps in young, literary, journalistic, and cultural fields. His critique would also be described as blatant overreach. But the reality of the epidemics one encounters in corrupt milieus is disgusting. It leads one to prefer isolation, with few exceptions, as when the writer finds himself forced to join some battles against overly insidious corruption.

Sometimes, I joke to myself that if I had written my frank opinion in published literary works, I would have become the enemy of all those competing enemies. They would even agree to unite to fight against me, postponing their own fights for later. Or maybe they would continue at their usual pace and set aside time when they could cooperate to fight their common enemy. This critic would become the lost wolf in their eyes.

Can lone wolves be tamed in an environment where extremism is on the rise? Will the West play the role of taming these supposed lost wolves, or will it push them to become more destructive, turning them into explosives that are hidden in plain sight, or maybe ship them off to the land of strife, wars, and flames in an East that is afflicted with its own illusions, rulers, and wealth?

How miserable it is to see some—or all—refugees as lone wolves that may pounce on their new societies, devour their goods, and destroy their structure at any moment. How miserable to see any incitement to sedition and hatred from the people living on this or that shore.

The Self in Distress and Love

I do not want my writing to settle debts. I do not want to write scandalous stories, even though the life around us is rife with scandals. I do not want to name people and thus expose their identities by showing the cards or practices they consider so clever, and by which they attain things, or self-esteem.

Novels give me a wide, free space to transmogrify many things, events, and ideas through characters, imbuing them so that this supposed fiction is one of the many masks I wear as a novelist, in this game of conceal and reveal. Yet to be direct and list their names, descriptions, and history—that, to me, would be an impulsive act of revenge. And I am someone who strives to alleviate and relieve any of the feelings of hatred that have accumulated over time, feeling that my travels have stored up in a remote corner of my memory and kept, trapped there.

Is biography, in a sense, restrictive?

Do I write with a need to expose myself and others before my inner mirrors and before readers, some of whom may be attracted to a certain kind of scandalous writing? Is writing, by analogy, the art of allegory through exaggeration, delusion, or accusation? Is it at all possible to combine writing and nudity in the context of simile and interview? Is there a similarity between the tools and goals of these two cases? Is it enough to describe each of them as art, so that they can be included in the field of human creativity? Does the writer become entirely naked when writing parts of his biography or when he slips parts of his biography into his works? Is there a connection between writing and nudity?

Talk about nudity is sometimes an indication of a coming scandal, whether implicit or explicit. In their attempts to criticize him, some would describe the writer as shameful for disclosing everything, as though darkness is what meets concealment, masking, and veiling.

We may wonder whether nudity reveals what is behind the mask, or whether there is anything left hidden after the writer has revealed his own nudity. This is a question that implies interpretations of literary and artistic masks, as well as references to reasons and motives that may contribute to crystallizing a robe of words to decorate nudity, or to furnish its artistic space with literary and artistic techniques.

The Peruvian writer Mario Vargas Llosa, winner of the 2010 Nobel Prize, said of the relationship between nudity and writing that writing is similar to the art of striptease. He went on to say that the narrative resembles, from a certain angle, a girl in the spotlight, taking off her clothes and revealing her hidden charms, bit by bit. He also believes that the writer expresses his intimacy publicly, through his literary output.

Vargas Llosa acknowledges the difference between the two types of nakedness, because what the writer shows of himself is not his hidden charms, as in the case of that girl. Instead, the writer reveals the demons that torment him and render him obsessive. The ugliest part of this is his longings, his sins, his grudges. Another difference, he believes, is that, in the art of striptease, a girl is dressed in the beginning and naked at the end. The matter is the other way around in the case of the novel: at first the novelist is naked, then he becomes dressed.

He confirms that the personal experiences that are initially the motivation for writing a story remain stealthily cloaked during the creative process, so that no one, often not even the writer himself, can, when he finishes his literary work, easily hear the covert heart that beats in that body of work he imagined. Vargas Llosa says, in Natasha Wimmer's translation, "Writing novels is the equivalent of what professional strippers do when they take off their clothes and exhibit their naked bodies on stage. The novelist performs the same acts in reverse. In constructing the novel, he goes through the motions of getting dressed, hiding the nudity in which he began under heavy, multicolored articles of clothing conjured up out of his imagination."

Argentine Luis Gruss, in his book *The Unreachable,* says that the act of journaling is a summoning of souls out of a sense of guilt. It can also be seen as a strange hypocrisy or a type of wager on the future of those some call "the future generations." In this context, it is his belief that journaling is generally a sign of weakness, for it analyzes the feelings but not the causes behind them. All of this could reflect the role the diary plays as a vessel containing all the bits and pieces, and as a bet on a strange and urgent future. Gruss says that "literature is the ultimate rallying cry of an existence marked by a double flame of life and death. Art, by definition, contradicts life. For inevitable reasons, it feeds on it. There is no other option, but in this particular paradox lies its authority."

Is nudity one of many tools that art and writing employ to investigate what is behind nudity itself? Could nudity be one of the writer's masks in the game of suggestion and synthesis?

It is no secret that nudity and writing are binaries that complement one another in furnishing the artistic space, keeping its flame burning, and making it inspirational and multifaceted. Here, I want biography neither to be a constraint, nor a trap of any kind.

I convince myself by saying, "Don't ask who hurt you, but look for a medicine to heal your wounds yourself." For time guarantees the healing of all wounds and the settling of all scores. But, to do so, you must busy yourself with ways to quench your instinct for revenge—this is what takes you away from the path of dreaming, hope, and work, and sets you on a course of endless struggle with yourself and your surroundings. You will feel yourself laden with burdens, and your thirst for revenge will keep growing, heavy in your heart and soul. We can only be freed from the scars of the soul by outgrowing them and searching for other methods of salvation.

From time to time, I feel useless. Unable to do anything. That's when I feel a void settle in and oppresses me. I feel alienated from myself, and I try to contain myself and come up with reasons to resist these feelings and push forward. I sharpen my spirit, and my desperate self grows more solid and stubborn than any attempts to strengthen and comfort it. I leave myself in the swing of hopelessness and futility, where there is nothing but emptiness. I think of those who have reached higher ranks in their fields, of those who have reached glory and fame in the world of writing, and then retired, isolated. I envy them their boldness and honesty.

It is not easy to regain your lost faith in the ideas in which you once believed, and in the people you once trusted. You must invent new ways to believe in yourself and your world. You might feel that you are standing naked in the midst of a thundering hurricane, in a field crowded with people. There, strangers quickly glance at you, but reject the burden of contemplating your situation. They don't concern themselves with whether your behavior is a form of insanity, of protest, or of something else.

I go out to the sea and shout at the top of my lungs. I feel a strange comfort that surprises me, so I release several more.

Haitham Hussein is a Kurdish-Syrian novelist born in Amouda in 1978 and now lives in London. He is a member of the Authors Society of Great Britain and a member of the Scottish PEN. He contributes to Arabic newspapers and is the founder of alriwaya.net, is the only website specializing in the contemporary Arabic fiction. His novel "Hostages of Sin" (2009, Damascus) was translated into Czech and published in 2016. It was also adapted into a play in Czech. Translated excerpts of "Hostages of Sin" appeared in an issue of the English-language magazine Banipal devoted to Syrian literature. Among Hussein's other novels, all published in Arabic, are "Aram: The Descendent of Unspoken Pains" (2006, Damascus); "Needle of Horror" (2013, Beirut and Algeria. It was translated into French, Paris 2020, by L'Armattan) and "A Weed in Paradise" (2017, Tunisia). He has published works of literary criticism: "The Novel between Mining and Puzzling" (Aleppo, 2011); "The Novel and the Life" (2013, UAE); "The Novelist Beats the Drums of War" (2014, Dubai); "The Fictional Character" (2015, UAE); "Why should You be a Novelist" (2020, Jordan) and edited "The Story of the First Novel by 30 Arab Novelists" (2017, Dubai)

Nicole Fares is a translator, writer and instructor, with a PhD in Comparative Literature and Cultural Studies and an MFA in Translation and Creative writing. She has worked with international human rights organizations, such as Amnesty International and The United Nations, and has translated four novels, including Mahmoud Shukair's Jerusalem Stands Alone and Sahar Mandour's 32, both of which have won prestigious translation awards. She has also written and translated for The New York Times, Cengage Learning, Syracuse University Press and World Literature Today. Her upcoming translation is Sahar Mandour's Vienna.